Hors d'Oeuvres

Hors d'Oeuvres

NORMAN KOLPAS

FRIEDMAN/FAIRFAX PUBLISHERS

A FRIEDMAN/FAIRFAX BOOK

Copyright © 1993 by Michael Friedman Publishing Group, Inc.

ISBN 1-56799-049-5

Editor: Stephen Williams
Designer: Judy Morgan
Senior Photography Editor: Christopher C. Bain
Photography Editor: Ede Rothaus

Typeset by Mar + x Myles Graphics, Inc.
Color separations by Universal Colour Scanning Ltd.
Printed in Hong Kong and bound in China by Leefung-Asco Printers Ltd.

Additional Photo Credits: © FPG International/Y. Miyazaki: p25, © FPG International/Bruce
Byers: p33, © FPG International/R. Thomas: p41, © FPG International/R. Thomas: p49,
© FPG International/D. Hallinan: p55, © Ron Goulet/Marvin Denbinsky Photo Associates: p63,
© FPG International/Bruce Byers: p71, © Sharon Guynup: p79, © Michael Grand: p81,
© Burke/Triolo: p84, © Bill Aron/Photo Edit: p86, © FPG International/Travel Pix: p89,
© FPG International/Ulf Sjostedt: p99, © Burke/Triolo: p103, © FPG International/Travel Pix:
p107, © Frank Whitney/The Image Bank: p117, © FPG International/Peter Johansky: p123,
© Jim Markham: p125, © FPG International/Al Michaud: p133

For bulk purchases and special sales, please contact:
Friedman/Fairfax Publishers
15 West 26 Street
New York, NY 10010
(212) 685-6610 FAX (212) 685-1307

Acknowledgements

My thanks to Michael Friedman and Karla Olson for proposing the original idea for this book, and to Stephen Williams for being a good-humored and steadfast editor.

My wife, Katie, deserves, as always, the largest measure of thanks—for her support and patience, her delight in entertaining and her spirited love of good food.

Contents

Contents

Hors d'oeuvres—the perfect name for appetizers, wonderful foods served outside (hors) the main work (oeuvre) of the meal. Hors d'oeuvres are friendly, carefree foods, created for pleasure. The foods we serve before the main meal are meant to entice, beguile and excite us.

It's no wonder, then, that a buffet table composed entirely of hors d'oeuvres has become a popular centerpiece at parties. Hors d'oeuvres can be easier to prepare than a full dinner menu. They allow you to invite more people and they offer tremendous variety to your guests. A party menu of hors d'oeuvres is like a three-ring (or, more often, a six-, seven- or eight-ring) circus—a selection of different dazzling acts competing for your attention simultaneously, each ready to delight you in its own way.

Hors d'Oeuvres celebrates appetizers in all their dazzling diversity. It begins with a concise discussion of the different ingredients that contribute to the appetizer table—the vegetables, meats and seafoods, cheeses, dips, spreads, breads and beverages that join together to make a display of bite-size delights. It

© FPG International/R. Chandler

then offers a step-by-step guide to planning your own appetizer party: from choosing the occasion and drawing up the guest list, through the preparation, organization, table setting and hassle-free cleanup.

The heart of the book is devoted to fourteen different appetizer party menus inspired by the seasons, the world's great cuisines and America's indigenous cooking styles. Each menu includes suggestions for setting the table and setting the mood, and every recipe offers guidelines for advance preparation and efficient cooking that will help you perform your job as host or hostess with the utmost efficiency.

Feel free to use the menus and guidelines exactly as they're set forth. But also feel free to let your imagination lead you. This book is intended to inspire you to create your own unique appetizer parties. Flip through the pages, from menu to menu, recipe to recipe, mixing, matching and changing what you find to suit your own tastes and whims. There are no hard and fast menu rules. Let this book be the starting point of hundreds of wonderful parties to come!

© Riccardo Marcialis/Photo Researchers

The Design of a Good Party

*T*he beauty of entertaining with an hors d'oeuvre buffet is that much of the food is prepared in advance and all of it is served at once, leaving you free to mingle with your guests and enjoy the party.

The challenge is to ensure that all those foods you're offering simultaneously are served at their peak and remain there as the party progresses.

The following simple strategies should help you throw a successful appetizer party with ease.

The Occasion

Before anything else, consider the occasion. Are you celebrating a holiday? An anniversary? A birthday? A promotion? A housewarming? Are you welcoming out-of-town visitors you want to introduce to a few of your friends? Or is it simply that you're looking for a good excuse to invite some people over whom you haven't seen in a while?

The occasion will dictate, to some extent, the style of your party—whether it should be an intimate gathering or a crowd; casual or formal; in the afternoon or evening; a simple or elaborate menu.

Sometimes, the foods themselves may even become the occasion. A daydream about an elegant caviar party or a Cajun feast is excuse enough to invite some friends over.

The Time

Hors d'oeuvres are intended to precede the evening meal. So most of the menus in this book were designed to be served during the predinner hours. If you've planned your party for a weekday evening, invite guests to come between 6 and 8, varying the times to accommodate local custom and rush hours.

On the weekend, you can start the party a little earlier if you like. And some menus in this book adapt themselves as well to other times of day. The Swedish Smorgasbord (page 99), for example, makes a pleasant weekend luncheon; the Rite of Spring menu (page 25) is ideal for a gathering on a sunny afternoon; the Russian Caviar Party (page 133) would seem even more sophisticated as a late-evening, after-theater event.

Though most of these menus are satisfying and won't leave your guests hungry, you might want to make it clear on the invitations that the event is for *hors d'oeuvres*, served from a *specific time* to a *specific time*. That way, none of your guests will be misled into thinking they're getting a sit-down meal, and they'll feel free to make plans for later in the evening.

The Guests

The people you invite are a major element of the party that often gets short shrift. The mix of guests can have as much of an effect on the success of a party as the foods you serve or the table you set. If they get along well and have sparkling conversations, they'll come away thinking they've had a great time; if they don't find each other fun

or interesting, no food or drink, no matter how good, will bail the party out.

This doesn't mean that you have to banish your less-than-scintillating friends forever from your home. Just bear in mind that the larger the crowd, the more opportunities there will be for people to find someone to chat with. So, especially for small gatherings, give careful thought to your guest list, imagining as best you can which people might click, adding someone to the list who you know has that special warmth and skill to bring out the shy-but-interesting person you're also inviting.

Incidentally, all of the menus in this book are easily multiplied or divided to accommodate the number of people you want to invite.

Be sure to give some thought to specific dietary requirements or personal tastes any of your guests might have. It's no use serving the Eastern Seaboard Elegance buffet (page 63) to people who are allergic to shellfish, for example; either change the guest list, or change the menu.

A Battle Plan

Once the occasion is set, the menu chosen and the guests invited, you've got to put on your general's hat and map out a strategy that will help you see the party through to a successful conclusion.

First, read all the recipes several times. Compile a shopping list and decide how you can buy the various ingredients in the fewest stops. Buy as much as you can in advance, reserving the purchase of perishables—such as raw oysters—for the day of the party.

As you compile your shopping list, draw up a time line to show how far in advance various stages of recipe preparation can be completed. Although you can make as

rough or polished a chart as suits you, it's a good idea to list the recipes down the left-hand side of the chart, and the time line—"three days before," "two days before," "one day before," "night before," "morning before," "three hours before," "one hour before," "last-minute"—along the top. Enter the various advance stages of recipe preparation onto this grid. It's also a good idea to note on the right-hand side of the chart which recipes are best prepared in batches so they can be enjoyed at their just-cooked peak. Tack the chart up on the kitchen wall or bulletin board. Then, at a glance, you'll be able to see what should be done when, and where you stand at any given moment in the party preparations.

You might also like to save room on the chart for adding any nonfood preparations: picking up rental glasses or a punchbowl for a large gathering; setting the table; picking up the flowers; retrieving the tablecloth from the cleaners; buying new records; and so on.

Setting the Appetizer Buffet Table

First, a word about the table itself. Most people today don't have a sideboard from which to serve appetizers. So the most common setting for an appetizer buffet is the dining-room table—which certainly offers plenty of room for presenting all the platters of food, the serving plates and various other accoutrements. But, depending on the size and style of the gathering, you could just as easily set up the buffet on the kitchen counter, the patio picnic table or a coffee table moved near the fireplace. And you can certainly move your table up against one wall if the layout of your home permits it, turning it into a large sideboard and leaving more room for guests to serve themselves and mingle.

Sample Recipe Planning Time Chart							
Recipes	*Two Days Before*	*One Day Before*	*Night Before*	*Several Hours Before*	*Last Minute*	**Amount**	**Batches**
1. Hummus			✔			4 cups	
2. Baba Ganoosh				✔		3 cups	
3. Taramasalata				✔		3 cups	
4. Pita Bread					✔		
5. Platter of Feta Cheese, Greek Olives, Tomatoes, Scallions					✔		
6. Tabbouleh on Baby Lettuce Leaves				✔		4 cups	
7. Grape Leaves Stuffed with Rice, Pine Nuts and Dill	✔						
8. Spinach and Feta Phyllo Triangles	✔					4 dozen	2–3
9. Fried Kibbeh Balls				✔	✔	4 dozen	several

Since most hors d'oeuvres are bite-size finger foods, the most important serving dish for your buffet table is the platter—square, rectangular, oval or round, with or without handles. Aim to have a separate serving platter for every recipe that requires one. Other items can also serve

the same purpose—a wooden cutting board, for example, or a marble pastry slab or, for small gatherings, a fairly large dinner plate.

To serve hot foods at their best, it's a good idea to present them on an electrically heated serving tray. Barring that, you can present them on a preheated oven-to-table platter placed on top of heat protecting pads or mats to protect the table. Or simply wrap the warm foods in a folded napkin on top of the platter.

Certain hot appetizers, such as Cheese Fondue (page 52), and Italian Bagna Cauda (page 76) will require a chafing dish or fondue pot to keep them warm at the table. Before the party be sure that you have enough of the right fuel for the heating element and that it's working properly.

Dishes meant to be served ice cold, such as Oysters on the Half Shell (page 66), can be set on a bed of crushed ice inside a large platter with a raised rim that will catch the water as it melts; a large, shallow bowl, such as a pasta serving bowl, will also do the trick.

Though most of the recipes in this book are meant to be eaten with the fingers, you should plan for the possibility that *all* your guests will be fastidious. Set out a stack of small, 5-to-7-inch plates on the buffet table, along with small appetizer or salad forks and folded cocktail napkins. Good quality paper napkins will also do nicely.

Depending on the size of the gathering and the size of your serving table or sideboard, you might want to put the drinks and glasses on a separate table. Keep any white wine you're pouring in an ice bucket and have more bottles chilled in the refrigerator. You can serve beer or soft drinks from the refrigerator; or present the bottles or cans in a large punch bowl filled with ice and water.

Setting a Style

In the menus that follow, you'll find suggestions for the styles of tableware—elegant silver and crystal, romantic floral patterns and rustic pottery—that will help set the mood for the menu and the occasion.

Of course, most people don't have fourteen or more different sets of dishes, platters and trays to play with, and it's likely that you'll be serving whatever menu you choose on whatever dishes you already have around the house.

But that doesn't mean that you can't create a mood for your party. Even one special platter—whether it's a family heirloom or something you go out and buy the morning of the party—can add just the right spirit to your buffet table. So can the other elements you add to your table: tablecloths, including old-world lace, ethnic-print fabrics and crisp, white linens; candles, whether stout and homey or tall, thin and elegant, with candlesticks to match; flowers, such as folksy daisies, riotous birds of paradise or a single aristocratic rosebud in a small crystal vase; and knickknacks, trinkets and collectibles, such as dolls, seashells, folk-art animals and pinecones. Let your imagination run wild in creating a table setting that expresses the mood you want.

And by all means add to that mood with music—whether you tune in the local jazz station or set a stack of your favorite old records on the turntable. Just be sure to keep the volume on the low side so that the music adds to the atmosphere without drowning out the conversation.

The Party in Progress

If you've done all the planning and plotting, your appetizer party should run smoothly. Before the appointed hour, make sure that you've set out all of your prepared dishes on the buffet table. Preheat the oven for anything that needs baking. If the menu calls for any deep-fried foods, preheat the oil in your skillet or deep fryer—keeping the skillet on a back burner to guard against dangerous spills, keeping children *out* of the kitchen and regulating the oil temperature carefully.

Once the first guests have been welcomed and given drinks, get the first batch of hot foods cooked and out on the table. Turn the heat under the oil way down so it doesn't get too hot; keep the oven temperature constant. Then enjoy the party for a while.

As the party progresses, keep checking the food on the table. When a platter of cold items starts looking a little bare, whisk it into the kitchen and set out a fresh, full platter. When the hot foods are running low, get some new batches going. Keep an eye on your guests' drinks too. Still, if the occasion allows it, set a sufficiently casual tone and encourage guests to help themselves to beverages as well as the food.

A Word on Help

If there aren't too many guests, all the aforementioned logistics can be easily handled by a single host—and even more easily if the host has a spouse or friend with whom to divide the duties.

But if the gathering is a larger one, don't go overboard. You won't have any fun. Hire some people to help you get everything ready a few hours before the party, help serve and help clear and clean up afterwards. Check your local yellow pages under Maid and Butler Services, Party Planning and Services, Bartenders and similar entries. Ask friends for suggestions on any good temporary help they've hired. Call up your local college or university and

© Bill Holden/Leo de Wys Inc.

ask if they have a student job-placement office that might put you in contact with some part-time workers. Nobody said that just because you're throwing a party you have to make it hard on yourself.

Cleanup

When it comes to cleanup, an appetizer party couldn't be easier. Since you'll have completed most of your preparation well in advance, most of the cleanup will already have been done, the pots and pans washed and put away.

As you're scanning the buffet table to check food levels during the party, also keep an eye out for any stray plates, forks or glasses that guests have finished with. Whisk them into the kitchen and stack them neatly in or near the sink. Do the same with empty food platters and with any utensils used in last-minute preparation the moment you're done with them.

Since the party should be over fairly early in the evening, there will be plenty of time to wash things up before exhaustion has set in. But, on the other hand, you may wish to spend the rest of the evening lingering with a few remaining guests or out on the town. With relatively few dishes to clean, and everything moved into the kitchen and neatly stacked, feel free to have what my wife and I refer to as a grown-up party. In other words, leave the final washing up and rearranging of furniture until the next morning. It's amazing how much easier cleanup tasks seem after a good night's sleep.

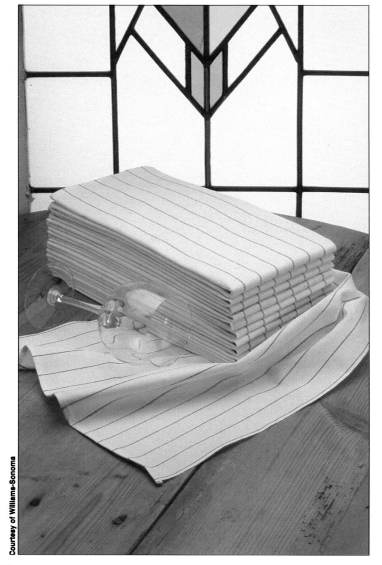

The Ingredients

*V*ariety is the spice of the appetizer table. The more wide ranging the tastes, textures, shapes and colors of the foods you offer your guests, the more memorable your party will be. Here's a quick guide that might give you good ideas for new ingredients. It also tells you how to get the highest quality foods.

In general, all of the ingredients in this book can easily be found in a good supermarket or delicatessen, although you may occasionally have to seek out specialty shops for some items. If you have limited access to good shopping, you might refer to the list of mail-order sources on page 140.

Vegetables and Fruits

Fresh produce brightens up virtually any appetizer selection. Vegetables and fruits lend color and texture to hors d'oeuvre stuffings. Sometimes they become containers for stuffings—lettuce cups hold Middle Eastern Tabbouleh (page 84), for example, or Mushrooms with Tasso and Bread Crumb Stuffing (page 123). Vegetables can even become the featured attraction, as in the platters of Fresh Spring Vegetables (page 28).

Although modern air freight and advanced growing techniques make most produce available year-round, you should still let seasonality dictate your purchases, leading you to the best-priced, freshest, most attractive vegetables and fruits available at any given time.

A particular delight for entertaining is the wide selection of specially raised baby vegetables now available in well-stocked supermarkets around the country. These are not only beautiful, and exquisitely flavored, they also meet one of the ideal requirements for hors d'oeuvre ingredients: they're already bite-size!

Seafood

Shellfish are among the best seafoods for hors d'oeuvre parties. The reason is simple: oysters, mussels and clams come in individual serving containers, each one offering a single, delectable bite. Oysters, in particular, are the height of elegance when served raw (see page 66). They, like the other shellfish, can also be blanketed with a stuffing and baked, as in the classic recipe, Oysters Rockefeller, on page 67.

Many people today are wary of shellfish, having heard tales of polluted waters. True, that danger does exist. Your best bet for ensuring that the shellfish you buy is in peak condition, and not tainted, is to purchase it from the most reputable seafood merchant you can find; if you don't know any personally, ask around—call up a good local restaurant that is famed for its shellfish and ask the chef where he or she shops for seafood. Above all, do *not* buy any shellfish that looks or smells at all suspicious; good seafood should look clean, bright and moist, and have a clean, clear, fresh smell of the sea, without any

19

unpleasant fishiness.

Another elegant seafood for the hors d'oeuvre table is caviar—the lightly processed and salted roe of sturgeon and other fish such as salmon, whitefish and lumpfish. (You'll find a complete discussion of caviar in the Russian Caviar Party on page 136.) Caviar can be the centerpiece of one of the most memorable parties you ever throw, or it can add a crowning touch to any buffet when used simply as a garnish, as in the Open-Faced Mini Sandwiches on page 104.

Shrimp are one of the most popular seafoods for hors d'oeuvres. Large raw shrimp that you buy in their shells will have the sweetest flavor and plumpest texture for bite-size, whole-shrimp appetizers. Tiny bay shrimp are perfect in appetizer stuffings and salads such as the Shrimp Remoulade on page 120. They are usually sold precooked at seafood counters; you can also use canned bay shrimp.

Smoked fish—particularly smoked salmon—is another indispensable hors d'oeuvre ingredient. Smoking heightens the naturally sweet flavor and voluptuous texture of salmon. Buy the best smoked salmon you can find, opting for fish thinly sliced off the fillet to order rather than for the presliced deli variety, which is coarser and oilier.

Poultry and Meat

In most cases, poultry and meat dishes served at the hors d'oeuvre table are simply smaller versions of entrée dishes, such as the Miniature Blue Cheese Burgers (page 36) or the Garlic Chicken (page 112) that's served as part of the Spanish Tapas buffet. So you should simply apply the same standards to the meat and poultry you buy for appetizers as you apply to meat and poultry for your main

© Burke/Triolo

courses—select the best grades and the freshest and leanest cuts available.

Many appetizers feature cured meats and poultry, such as salted or smoked hams and sausages. Sometimes they're blended in to flavor a recipe; other times, they are a dish in their own right, served in attractively overlapping slices on an appetizer platter. Particular varieties are described in various recipes throughout this book, from Cajun andouille (page 123) to Italian prosciutto (page 76). You'll get your best education in the variety of cured meats available for the buffet table on a trip to your local deli; peruse what's available, ask about any you aren't familiar with and taste them. You might be surprised at what you find.

Cheeses

Many people feel that cheese and crackers are the only appetizers they need to serve. The richness and tang of a good piece of cheese does perk up the appetite amazingly, and you'll find a variety of cheeses—blues and bries, Cheddars and chevres, Gruyères and mozzarellas—doing just that throughout this book. But cheeses can also be served in more imaginative ways.

Cheeses can be seasonings and stuffings, such as the feta that joins spinach in the Spinach and Feta Phyllo Triangles (page 86) or the grated Parmesan in Oysters Rockefeller (page 67). Cheese also plays a starring role in the Winter Fondue Buffet (page 49) and the Pacific Coast Pizza Party (page 55).

Many supermarkets today have marvelously varied cheese sections, and gourmet food shops and delicatessens in most good-size cities and towns stock an even greater selection.

© Burke/Triolo

Dips, Dressings, Spreads and Sauces

Different ingredients contribute their unique characters to the dips, dressings, spreads and sauces that grace most hors d'oeuvre tables.

Preeminent among these is olive oil, which is used not only as a cooking oil for sautéing, but also as a flavoring agent and an element in salad dressings and marinades. Buy only olive oil labeled "extra-virgin." That means it was extracted from the fruit on the first pressing, without the use of heat or chemicals. It will have the pure, clean, fruity taste of good olives. Many different brands of olive oil are available today in supermarkets and gourmet shops, and their color may vary from pale gold to dark green, with flavors ranging correspondingly from light to heavy and fruity. I personally opt for darker oils, only because I like their pronounced olive taste; choose one that you like. (Use a flavorless, cholesterol-free vegetable oil for deep frying. Be sure to use fresh oil every time you deep fry, to ensure clean-tasting, nongreasy fried foods.)

Whenever I use butter in this book, I call for unsalted (sweet) butter. This makes it possible to salt dishes to taste.

Sour cream, a mainstay of dips, is being replaced in fashionable dining establishments these days by crème fraîche—the lightly–fermented French heavy cream. You'll find crème fraîche in the dairy or cheese cases of many upscale supermarkets and delis. If you can't find it, you can make an acceptable substitute by lightly whipping one part of heavy cream and then combining it with three parts of sour cream.

When recipes call for mayonnaise, it is perfectly acceptable to use the best brand of commercial mayonnaise you can buy.

© Burke/Triolo

Breads and Crackers

Sourdough, pumpernickel, rye and whole-wheat breads all play their part at some time or other on an appetizer buffet table, whether they are cut into bite-size portions or served as miniature cocktail loaves. Find a good local baker, or a supermarket that stocks a quality selection of fresh breads.

Likewise, explore the cracker aisle of your local market for a selection of crisp bases for meats, cheeses and spreads. A word of caution: don't be swayed by the latest, snazzily flavored marketing gimmicks. Go for the classics—good water biscuits, cream crackers, whole-wheat biscuits and so on.

Drinks

I've suggested appropriate drinks—alcoholic and non-alcoholic—with every menu in this book. I'd like to observe here that, despite trendy magazine articles that say that *this* hard liquor or *that* hard liquor is being con-sumed like never before, the real movement today is decidedly in the direction of softer alcoholic drinks for appetizer entertaining—white and light red wines, beer and sparkling water. (And I say that as a man who enjoys a good martini from time to time.)

Stock your home bar if you and your guests are so inclined; and if you're throwing a huge wingding with dozens of guests, you may well want to hire a bartender for the evening to mix cocktails to order. But I find that an appetizer party goes much more smoothly if you inte-grate your drink selection into the menu. Pour something that best complements the selection of foods, but still offer a few alternatives to guests who don't want to drink the main selection.

© Steven Mark Needham/Envision

23

Rite of Spring

What better way to celebrate the season of rebirth than with a resplendent array of garden-fresh vegetables and fruits? The following hors d'oeuvre buffet could hardly be easier to prepare, featuring as it does a selection of quickly prepared, raw or barely cooked produce and easily mixed dips and dressings. Simple as it is, it's wonderfully suitable for a large, casual gathering on a weekend afternoon when the weather has begun to warm up (and it's a great party, with some seasonal variations, to host all through the summer). You can easily reduce the portions for smaller groups, or even double or triple them when you expect many guests.

Serve the prepared vegetables and fruits from country baskets or rustic pottery; include a few whimsical serving pieces with a fruit or vegetable motif, if you have them. Use smaller rather than larger serving ware, to give a bounteous effect. Let the natural wood of a country table or sideboard show through; or cover your tables with coarse linen, a floral print cloth or gingham checks. Set out small plates for guests, and, though there's no real need, forks for those who'd like to use them. Put some easy folk, light jazz or classical music on the stereo.

27

M E N U

Platters of Fresh Spring Vegetables

Herbed Crème Fraîche

Toasted Onion Dip

Platters of Fresh Fruits

Honey-Lime-Mint Yogurt Dip

Assorted Cheeses, Breads and Crackers

White Wines and Sparkling Waters

Serves 24

© Burke/Triolo

Platters of Fresh Spring Vegetables

The selection of vegetables you set out need only be limited by what's available and good at your local supermarket or greengrocer.

Aim to serve about 1/2 pound of vegetables total per guest, presenting about six vegetables from the following list. Choose the smallest, freshest vegetables, and reject produce that looks anything less than perfect. Prepare and arrange the vegetables 2 to 3 hours in advance and refrigerate them, covered.

Asparagus—The youngest, tenderest, pencil-thin asparagus may be served raw, its stem ends trimmed. Otherwise, parboil asparagus in plenty of boiling water until tender-crisp (about 1 minute, depending on size); drain immediately and rinse under cold running water; chill in the refrigerator until serving.

Belgian endive—Buy the small, pale-yellow-to-white heads and separate the leaves. Rinse in cold running water and pat them dry.

Broccoli—Cut the heads into bite-size florets. Leave raw; or, if you prefer, parboil in plenty of water until tender-crisp, about 2 minutes, then rinse under cold running water until cool. Either way, chill in the refrigerator before serving.

Cauliflower—Cut the head into bite-size florets. Leave raw; or, if you prefer, parboil the florets in plenty of water until tender-crisp, about 2 minutes, then rinse them under cold running water until cool. Either way, chill cauliflower in the refrigerator before serving.

Celery—Cut the ribs lengthwise into sticks about 1/4 to 1/2 inch wide and 4 inches long. Chill in ice water.

Cucumbers—Peel chilled cucumbers, leaving narrow strips of green, if you like, for a decorative effect, and then slice straight or at a 45-degree angle into 1/4-inch-thick slices. Small pickling cucumbers need not be peeled and can be cut lengthwise in halves or quarters.

Fennel—Trim this anise-flavored bulb and slice it about 1/4 inch thick, cutting the slices into halves or sticks. Chill in ice water.

Jicama—Peel to remove any trace of the brown skin or woody exterior; cut the crisp flesh into sticks about 1/4 to 1/2 inch wide and 3 to 4 inches long. Chill in ice water.

Lettuces—Select baby lettuce leaves or hearts of larger lettuces—such as Boston, Bibb, butter, romaine and red leaf. Separate the leaves, wash well, pat dry and chill in the refrigerator until serving.

Mushrooms—Select small to medium white cultivated mushrooms. Trim away any dirty or ragged stems. Wipe the caps clean with a damp cloth or paper towel—do not wash with water.

Peppers—Halve, stem, seed and rib bell peppers—red, green, yellow, orange and purple—and cut them into strips 1/2 to 1 inch wide. Chill in ice water.

© Envision

Radicchio—Separate the leaves, wash well, pat dry and chill in the refrigerator.

Radishes—Trim off all but about 1/4 to 1/2 inch of each radish's stem. Chill in ice water.

Scallions—Buy the smallest you can find. Trim off the roots and any ragged green tips. Chill in ice water.

Snow peas—Trim and string the pods. Parboil in plenty of water until tender-crisp, 30 seconds to 1 minute, depending on size; rinse under cold running water until cool. Chill in the refrigerator before serving.

Spinach—Separate the spinach into individual leaves, trimming the stems. Wash in several changes of cold water, lifting the leaves out each time before you drain the water, until not a trace of sand or dirt remains; pat the leaves dry.

© Envision

String beans—Trim and string large beans; leave the stems on tiny beans for a decorative effect. Parboil in plenty of boiling water until tender-crisp, 1 to 2 minutes, depending on size, then drain immediately. Rinse under cold running water until cool; chill in the refrigerator.

Tomatoes—Serve small, chilled, bite-size red cherry or orange tomatoes with their stems still attached.

Watercress—Separate the watercress into bite-size clusters; wash well; chill in the refrigerator.

Zucchini—Cut green or yellow zucchini into sticks or spears 1/4 to 1/2 inch wide or at a 45-degree angle into 1/4-inch-wide ovals. Rinse the pieces briefly under cold running water, then pat dry and chill in the refrigerator.

Herbed Crème Fraîche

This may be mixed 2 to 3 hours ahead of time. Serve this dip and the following one alongside vegetables in a bowl lined with lettuce leaves. Or, for a striking presentation, serve it in a hollowed-out cabbage. Trim the base of the cabbage flat to make it steady; then, with a small, sharp knife, carefully carve a bowl-like hollow in the top of the cabbage.

5 cups crème fraîche (or 3 cups sour cream, drained and mixed with 1 cup lightly whipped heavy cream)

1/4 cup chopped fresh basil

1/4 cup chopped fresh chives

1/4 cup chopped fresh dill

1/4 cup chopped fresh parsley

2 tablespoons lemon juice

1 small sweet onion (Vidalia, Walla Walla or Maui), finely chopped

Salt and freshly ground white pepper

In a mixing bowl, stir together all the ingredients until thoroughly blended, seasoning to taste. Chill in the refrigerator.

Makes about 6 cups

Toasted Onion Dip

A sophisticated version of the old packaged favorite.

6 cups thinly sliced onions

1 tablespoon salt

3 cups vegetable oil

3 cups sour cream, drained of excess liquid

2 tablespoons Worcestershire sauce, or to taste

1/4 cup chopped fresh chives

In a large mixing bowl, toss the onions with the salt and let stand for about 5 minutes.

A few handfuls at a time, gently squeeze the onions between double thicknesses of paper towels to remove excess moisture.

In a large wok or skillet, heat the oil over medium to low heat. Add the onions and fry them, stirring frequently, until light golden brown, about 7 minutes. Remove them with a wire skimmer, and let them drain and cool on paper towels.

You may fry the onions several hours ahead of time, if you like. Shortly before serving, crumble the onions into the sour cream and stir until blended. Season to taste with 1 to 2 tablespoons of Worcestershire sauce and garnish with chives.

Makes about 6 cups

Platters of Fresh Fruits

You don't need to do anything but arrange bite-size portions of the most beautiful, best-tasting fruits you can find on the day of your party—whole berries, firm chunks of ripe melon, orange segments, nectarine and peach slices and little baby plums would all be perfect.

It's best not to put sliced fruits together on the same platter since you could wind up with a messy mingling of juices; instead, place each on a separate dish. You can do this an hour or so ahead of time and refrigerate them, covered. Arrange the whole fruits in baskets or bowls nearby to show them off. Accompany the sliced fruit with lemon or lime wedges so guests can squeeze them over the fruit.

Honey-Lime-Mint Yogurt Dip

Serve this sweet-tart dip alongside the fruit. Though it tastes richest when made with whole-milk yogurt and cream, you can certainly make it with low-fat yogurt.

5 cups yogurt

1/2 cup lightly whipped heavy cream

1/2 cup honey, at room temperature

1/4 cup finely chopped fresh mint leaves

3 tablespoons lime juice

Fresh mint sprigs for garnish

In a mixing bowl, stir together the yogurt, cream, honey, chopped mint and lime juice until thoroughly blended. Chill, covered, in the refrigerator. Garnish with mint sprigs before serving.

Makes about 6 cups

Assorted Cheeses, Breads and Crackers

Select a variety of cheeses to complement the fresh tastes and textures of the vegetables and fruits—a ripe, creamy brie or Camembert; a crumbly Roquefort or other blue-veined cheese; a heavy, tangy Swiss or Gruyère; a sharp Cheddar; a rich, spreadable garlic-herb cheese such as Boursin™; and anything else that may strike your fancy. Allow about 1/4 pound of cheese per person.

Present the cheeses on a platter covered with grapevine leaves, lettuces or other fresh foliage. Alongside them, present a basket of coarsely sliced fresh sourdough and black bread, and assorted crackers such as English water biscuits, Middle Eastern *lavash* and Scandinavian rye crisps. For those who would like it, include a dish of softened unsalted butter.

White Wines and Sparkling Waters

Offer your guests two different white wines with these fresh springtime hors

© Guy Gillette/Photo Researchers

d'oeuvres: a crisp, dry sauvignon blanc to complement the vegetables and a light, fruity chardonnay to go with the fruits. Serve both wines well chilled.

Have a good supply of sparkling water on hand for guests who don't want to drink. Many brands now offer varieties lightly flavored with fruit essences but free of sweeteners; these would go very well with the fruits. Be prepared to mix spritzers—one or two parts of white wine to one part of sparkling water—for guests who want a very light aperitif; serve them in tall glasses over ice, with a small wedge of lime or lemon.

*A Summer
Cookout*

Fire up the grill for this easy summertime appetizer buffet, featuring miniature versions of some traditional warm-weather favorites.

The featured foods can easily be prepared in advance, so they're ready to cook once guests arrive. Start your barbecue fire a good hour ahead of time, so the coals are glowing red-hot when the party starts. And even if you're an apartment dweller without a terrace, you can simply cook on an indoor grill or broiler, though you may have to cut the number of guests in half because of limited cooking capacity.

There's no need here for special dishes that you'll have to clean up when you could be enjoying the warm weather. Though you'll need some good, simple serving platters for the food, paper plates are best for the guests, especially the decorative plastic-coated variety; if you'd like to give them added support, look for wicker paper-plate holders, which are available in many supermarkets and kitchen stores. Paper napkins are perfectly acceptable as well, along with good-size plastic cutlery—not the hard-to-use small stuff. You can even use paper cups, though the Bloody Marys look their best in real highball glasses. Outdoors or in, cover the table with a gingham checked cloth.

35

M E N U

Miniature Blue Cheese Burgers

Barbecued Chicken Kebabs

Grilled Marinated Shrimp

Grilled Vegetables

Bloody Marys

Serves 16

Miniature Blue Cheese Burgers

Assemble the cheese-stuffed burgers 2 to 3 hours in advance and refrigerate them on a wax paper–lined tray, covered with another sheet of wax paper, until it's time to cook them. Then cook the burgers in several batches.

A good bakery should have cocktail egg or onion rolls about 3 inches in diameter to use as burger buns.

Be sure to set out your favorite condiments—sliced sweet onions, relish, ketchup and good grainy mustard—for guests to put on their burgers.

5 pounds lean ground beef

1 medium onion, minced

2 medium garlic cloves, minced

1/2 cup finely chopped fresh parsley

1 1/2 pounds creamy blue cheese, mashed

Vegetable oil

Salt and freshly ground black pepper

40 cocktail rolls, split

In a mixing bowl, thoroughly blend the beef, onion, garlic and parsley. Divide the mixture into 40 equal balls, each weighing about 2 ounces.

Measure out 40 separate level table-spoons of the cheese, moistening your hands and shaping them into even balls. Holding a ball of beef in your hand, press a ball of cheese into its center, shaping the meat around the cheese to surround it completely. Flatten the ball into a plump burger shape about 3¹/₂ inches in diameter.

Preheat the barbecue, grill or broiler until very hot. Brush the burgers lightly with oil and season with salt and pepper. Cook the burgers 3 to 5 minutes per side. Serve them on split rolls.

Makes 40 burgers

Barbecued Chicken Kebabs

Make the barbecue sauce the night before. Assemble the kebabs and start marinating them 2 to 3 hours before guests arrive. Barbecue them in several batches, arranging them on a serving tray.

2 tablespoons corn oil

2 medium garlic cloves, finely chopped

1 small onion, finely chopped

1 sixteen-ounce can tomato puree

1/4 cup molasses

3 tablespoons dark brown sugar

3 tablespoons malt vinegar

2 teaspoons dried oregano

1 teaspoon salt

1 teaspoon chili powder

3/4 teaspoon liquid natural hickory seasoning

3¹/₂ pounds boneless, skinless chicken breast, cut into 1-inch pieces

Heat the oil in a medium saucepan over medium heat. Add the garlic and onion and sauté 3 to 5 minutes, until transparent. Add the remaining sauce ingredients, bring to a light boil, reduce the heat and simmer about 10 minutes, until thick. Cool to room temperature, then refrigerate, covered.

Thread 2 or 3 cubes of chicken on each of 40 small bamboo skewers. Arrange the skewers in a shallow dish and pour the sauce over them. Cover and marinate in the refrigerator for 2 to 3 hours, turning the kebabs several times in the sauce.

Preheat the barbecue, grill or broiler until very hot. Cover the ends of the skewers with small pieces of foil to prevent bamboo from charring. Cook the kebabs close to the heat about 4 minutes per side or until done, basting with the sauce.

Makes 40 kebabs

© FPG International/Peter Johansky

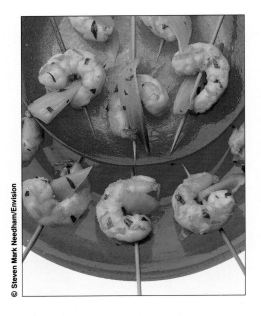

© Steven Mark Needham/Envision

Grilled Marinated Shrimp

If your barbecue grill is so widely spaced that the shrimp can fall through, thread the shrimp on skewers for cooking, then slip them off the skewers onto the serving platter.

5 pounds (about 80) medium shrimp

1 cup olive oil

1/2 cup lemon juice

1 tablespoon dried oregano

1/2 tablespoon dried rosemary

1/2 tablespoon dried thyme

Salt and freshly ground white pepper

Carefully peel and devein the shrimp, leaving their tails on. (To devein a shrimp, first peel it and then use a small, sharp knife to make a shallow incision along its back, or outer curve; remove the vein that is just under the surface.)

Put the shrimp in a large mixing bowl with the olive oil, lemon juice and herbs. Toss well to coat them, then cover with plastic wrap and refrigerate for 1 hour.

Preheat the barbecue, grill or broiler until very hot. Season the shrimp with salt and white pepper and cook them close to the heat for 1 to 2 minutes per side, until done.

Makes about 80 shrimp hors d'oeuvres

Grilled Vegetables

An assortment of grilled vegetables makes a wonderful accompaniment to the other appetizers. Up to two hours in advance, have the vegetables trimmed and ready to grill in batches.

32 medium scallions, trimmed

32 large mushrooms, wiped clean and stemmed

16 medium (5 to 6 inches) zucchini, trimmed and halved lengthwise

16 medium (5 to 6 inches) yellow summer squash (golden zucchini), trimmed and halved lengthwise

8 fennel bulbs, trimmed

16 small Japanese eggplants, trimmed and halved lengthwise

Olive oil

Salt and freshly ground black pepper

Preheat the barbecue, grill or broiler until very hot.

Just before putting them on the grill, brush the vegetables generously all over with olive oil and sprinkle them with salt and pepper. Grill the vegetables until they are lightly charred and cooked through, 2 to 4 minutes per side, depending on size and kind of vegetable. Transfer them to a serving platter.

Bloody Marys

Mix up the base in two batches as the party proceeds. If the people you invite dislike spicy drinks, reduce the amounts of horseradish and Tabasco™. Naturally, you can also make the drinks "virgin" if you like. Either way, be sure there are plenty of ice cubes in your freezer to chill the Bloody Marys.

Have soft drinks, sparkling water, wine and beer on hand, too.

6 *quarts tomato juice*

1 *cup Worcestershire sauce*

2 *tablespoons grated horseradish*

1/2 *to 1 teaspoon Tabasco™ sauce*

1/2 *cup fresh lemon juice*

Salt

2 *quarts vodka*

32 *celery stalks, untrimmed*

32 *lemon wedges*

For each batch, stir together 3 quarts of tomato juice, 1/2 cup of Worcestershire, 1 tablespoon of horseradish, some Tabasco™ and 1/4 cup of lemon juice. Season to taste with salt (the saltiness of the tomato juice may vary from brand to brand).

Fill highball glasses with ice cubes and add 1 to 2 ounces of vodka, depending on how strong each guest wants the drink. Fill the rest of the way with the tomato juice mixture (stir it up again just before pouring). Add a celery stalk as a swizzle stick, and give the drink a quick stir to mix the vodka and juice. Garnish with a lemon wedge.

Makes 32 six-ounce drinks

A Cozy
Fall Buffet

As the nights get longer and the days grow cool, plan this
celebration of comforting, hearty foods, featuring freshly baked,
old-fashioned, bite-size biscuits and an array of satisfying
fixings: a good-quality Country Ham with Honey Mustard; Chicken or
Turkey à la King; Zesty Salmon Spread; a selection of full-flavored
cheeses; and Mulled Cider.

Set your table in fall colors—earth tones, warm reds and bright
oranges—and, if trees are close at hand, gather up a selection of attractive,
clean, fallen leaves in varied hues to scatter between the serving dishes.
Add other rustic touches, like a basket lined with a checked napkin for the
biscuits, perhaps, or pewter candlesticks, pinecones or evergreen boughs.

This is a flexible hors d'oeuvre buffet because it is hearty enough to
make a good lunch or an early evening meal. Although folk or classical
music would be a pleasant accompaniment, this food may be best suited
for televised sports, the World Series or a good football game. Choose the
entertainment that best suits your guests.

43

M E N U

Whole-Wheat Buttermilk Beaten Biscuits

Country Ham

Honey Mustard

Zesty Salmon Spread

Cheese Platter with Apples

Chicken or Turkey à la King

Mulled Cider

Serves 12

Whole-Wheat Buttermilk Beaten Biscuits

At one time old-fashioned biscuit dough had to be beaten by hand for over half an hour with a rolling pin or even a hammer! But these days the dough takes just a few minutes to prepare with a food processor, and the biscuits can be popped in the oven moments before guests arrive.

Bake them in several batches, and keep them warm in a napkin-lined basket. The biscuits are easily split in two with your fingertips, to be spread with soft butter or filled with ham, turkey or chicken à la king, cheese or salmon spread.

4 cups all-purpose flour

1 1/3 cup whole-wheat flour

2 1/2 teaspoons salt

1 1/4 cups unsalted butter, cut into pieces

2 cups cold buttermilk

Preheat the oven to 350°.

Place dry ingredients in a food processor fitted with the metal blade and turn the machine on and off a few times to mix. Add the butter, and process until the mixture resembles coarse cornmeal.

With the processor running, gradually add about 1 1/2 cups of the buttermilk. Continue processing, adding more buttermilk if necessary, until the dough forms a ball that rides around the bowl on the blade. Process continuously for 2 minutes more.

On a lightly floured surface, press out the dough with your hands in a rough rectangle about 1/8 inch thick. Fold the dough in half and gently press down. With a floured, 1 1/2-to-2-inch cookie cutter (or an inverted glass), cut the dough into biscuits, placing them 1/2 to 1 inch apart on an ungreased baking sheet. Gather up the scraps, flatten and fold them again, and repeat until all the dough is used up.

Bake the biscuits 25 to 30 minutes, until golden. Serve in a napkin-lined basket. Show your guests how easily the biscuits can be split by hand and filled.

Makes about 8 dozen

Country Ham

Such good hams are so widely available today that there's no point going to the trouble of baking one yourself for a casual party. Buy a good precooked one that has been smoked over aromatic wood and cured or baked with spices and sweeteners—a Smithfield or other Virginia ham, a Vermont cob-smoked ham or whatever tastes best at your local deli.

Allow at least 1/4 pound of ham—not counting the bone—per person, but don't hesitate to buy more and keep any left-overs for future meals. If you can, save yourself and your guests the trouble of carving and have the deli preslice the ham on the bone; just a neat bit of cutting next to the bone at the party will free each slice in turn. The sliced ham can be stored in the refrigerator until you are ready to serve it.

Honey Mustard

You may mix this several hours in advance. Set this sweet mustard out in a rustic crockery pot to spread on the biscuits with the ham.

3/4 cup grainy, Dijon-style mustard

1/4 cup honey, at room temperature

In a mixing bowl, stir together the mustard and honey until blended. Store any extra in an airtight container in the refrigerator.

Makes about 1 cup

Zesty Salmon Spread

Make this mixture several hours before the party and refrigerate it covered. If you like, you can serve it in a country crock; or pack it into a lightly oiled decorative mold, and then unmold it onto a serving platter and garnish it with fresh dill or watercress sprigs.

As an alternative to biscuits, you can offer guests rounds of crisp cucumber to spread it on.

3 seven-ounce cans salmon, drained, bones and skin removed

3/4 pound cream cheese, at room temperature

3 tablespoons lemon juice

2 tablespoons Worcestershire sauce

1/4 teaspoon Tabasco™ sauce

1/4 cup chopped fresh parsley

Lemon wedges

Fresh dill or watercress sprigs

Place the salmon, cream cheese, lemon juice, Worcestershire and Tabasco™ in a food processor fitted with the metal blade. Process until smooth, stopping once or twice to scrape down the bowl. Pulse in the parsley.

Chill in a serving crock or lightly oiled decorative mold. Remove from the refrigerator 30 minutes before serving. Unmold, if necessary. Garnish with lemon wedges and dill or watercress sprigs.

Makes about 4 cups

© Ken Scott/Marvin Dembinsky Photo Associates

Cheese Platter with Apples

Set out a platter or wooden carving board with large blocks of robust cheeses—a sharp Cheddar, a ripe blue, some sort of smoked cheese (Gouda, Cheddar or mozzarella, for example), a tangy Swiss. Allow about ¼ pound of cheese per person.

On the same platter, or in a basket alongside, offer a selection of the best autumn apples, each one polished to a bright sheen with a clean kitchen towel. Count on each guest eating at least one apple, but buy twice as many as you need, for a look of harvest abundance.

Set out some sturdy, sharp knives for the cheeses and apples.

Chicken or Turkey à la King

Start preparing this classic dish 30 to 45 minutes before guests arrive, and keep it warm at the table in a chafing dish, ready to be spooned over split biscuits.

1/4 cup unsalted butter

1 medium onion, finely chopped

1 medium garlic clove, finely chopped

1/4 cup all-purpose flour

1 cup canned chicken broth

1 cup half-and-half

1 egg yolk

3 cups cooked chicken or turkey, cut into 1/2-inch cubes

1 medium red bell pepper, stemmed, seeded and cut into 1/4-inch pieces

1/2 cup cooked fresh or frozen peas

1/4 cup finely chopped fresh parsley

Salt and freshly ground black pepper

Grated nutmeg

In a large saucepan, melt the butter over medium-low heat. Add the onion and garlic and sauté until transparent. Sprinkle in the flour and cook, stirring, about 1 minute more.

Stirring constantly with a wire whisk, gradually add the broth and half-and-half. Raise the heat to medium and stir occasionally until the liquid comes to a boil. Reduce the heat and simmer gently about 10 minutes longer.

Beat the egg yolk until smooth. Stirring continuously, add a ladleful of the hot liquid into the egg yolk. Then, stirring continuously, gradually pour the mixture back into the saucepan. Reduce the heat to low, stir in the chicken or turkey and the bell pepper and peas and simmer about 5 minutes more, until they're well heated. Stir in the parsley, season to taste with salt and pepper and, if you like, add just a pinch of nutmeg.

To serve, spoon the mixture onto split biscuits.

Makes about 6 cups

Mulled Cider

Go ahead and offer your guests beer, wine and soft drinks with this hors d'oeuvre buffet. But for an authentic autumn touch, have a large pot of cider mulling in the kitchen, ready to ladle into heavy mugs right from the stove or to transfer to a heated punch bowl on the serving table. The cider and spices will perfume your whole home.

You can make this a hard cider, or omit the brandy and serve nonalcoholic cider if you prefer. Or split the recipe and offer your guests a choice of hard or soft.

1 1/2 gallons apple cider

1/2 cup raisins

6 cinnamon sticks, broken into 1-inch pieces

2 teaspoons whole cloves

Zest of 2 medium oranges, cut into thin strips

Zest of 1 medium lemon, cut into thin strips

1 cup brandy (optional)

Whole cinnamon sticks, for garnish

Put the cider, raisins, broken cinnamon sticks, cloves and orange and lemon zests into a large pot. Cook over medium heat until the mixture is hot but not yet boiling; reduce the heat to low and let the mixture steep, covered, for at least 15 minutes.

Before serving, stir in the brandy if you like. Ladle into heavy mugs and garnish each serving with a whole cinnamon stick.

Makes about 1 1/2 gallons

© Steven Mark Needham/Envision

A Winter
Fondue Buffet

W inter's chill seems to make us all seek comfort—in baggy clothes that cover us like blankets, in blazing fires that set our skins glowing and in simple, satisfying foods.

Among winter's most satisfying dishes is fondue, the melted cheese dish that originated centuries ago in the land of dairy products and snowy peaks, Switzerland, and has since come to be an international favorite. What's more, it's quickly prepared and easily served as the main attraction of an appetizer buffet, leaving you, the host, plenty of time to enjoy the warm companionship of your guests.

Set up the fondue table near the fireplace, if you have one. In any case, turn the lights down low and decorate the room with plenty of glowing candles. All you need in the way of serving dishes is a large fondue pot, chafing dish or flameproof casserole and assorted bowls and platters to hold the foods that will be dipped. Set out long-handled forks for your guests, along with small plates on which they can place dipped morsels en route to their mouths. Put on a recording of the warmest music you know, be it folk, classical or jazz, and enjoy an incomparably easy appetizer party.

51

M E N U

Cheese Fondue

Bread Cubes and Bread Sticks

Herbed Garlic Croutons

Sausage Chunks

Fresh Mushrooms

Pickled Cucumbers

Assorted Beers and Wines

Serves 8

Cheese Fondue

This fondue blends the two most distinctive Swiss cheeses: strong, sweet and nutty Gruyère and milder, mellower Emmentaler. If you can't locate one of them, make the fondue entirely with the other; or substitute the best-quality Swiss cheese you can find.

Assemble the ingredients up to 1 hour in advance and start cooking the fondue when your first guests arrive.

1 large garlic clove, cut in half

3 cups dry white wine

2 pounds Gruyère cheese, shredded

1 pound Emmentaler cheese, shredded

2 tablespoons cornstarch

3 tablespoons kirsch

1 tablespoon lemon juice

1/4 teaspoon freshly ground black pepper

1/4 teaspoon grated nutmeg

1/4 teaspoon salt

Thoroughly rub the inside of a fondue pot, chafing dish or flameproof casserole with the cut sides of the garlic clove; discard the garlic. Add the wine to the pot and heat over medium heat until hot but not boiling.

In a mixing bowl, toss the shredded cheeses with the cornstarch until the shreds are evenly dusted. Add the cheese to the wine in the pot, reduce the heat to low and cook, stirring continuously, until the cheese melts and the mixture is thick and creamy. Stir in the kirsch, lemon juice and seasonings, then transfer the pot to the serving table and keep it warm over a spirit burner.

Serve with assorted bread cubes and other foods for dipping.

Makes 6 cups

Bread Cubes and Bread Sticks

Fondue is traditionally served with a crusty French bread that is good and firm. But you might also like to offer your guests alternatives: a dense, black raisin bread; a tangy sourdough; rye bread; whole-wheat bread; or whatever other quality loaves are available and taste good to you.

Buy 2 good-size, unsliced loaves of bread. Cut them into rough 1-inch chunks for dipping and pile them in bowls or napkin-lined baskets.

If you have a good deli nearby that stocks Italian products, you might also want to buy a few packages of crisp bread sticks—not the pencil-thin variety but the thicker kind. These are delightful dipped by hand into the fondue.

Herbed Garlic Croutons

As an alternative to simple bread chunks, you might want to also offer your guests these crisp, rustic croutons. Prepare them a few hours in advance and keep them crisp in an airtight container.

1/2 pound unsalted butter, cut into pieces

1/4 cup olive oil

2 medium garlic cloves, unpeeled but smashed

1 loaf French bread, cut into 1-inch cubes

1 teaspoon each dried oregano, thyme and rosemary

Preheat the oven to 400°.

Put the butter, oil and garlic in a skillet and cook over medium heat until the butter begins to foam. Remove and discard the garlic.

Put the bread cubes in a large mixing bowl. Drizzle them evenly with about one third of the butter-oil mixture and toss well with a pair of spoons or forks; drizzle with another third and toss again; then drizzle with the last third and toss again. Finally, crumble the herbs over the bread cubes and toss well again.

Place the bread cubes on a large baking tray and bake, turning them several times, about 30 minutes, until deep golden brown. Let them cool, then store them in an airtight container.

Sausage Chunks

Cheese and salami are natural partners. So, for a change of pace, offer your guests a bowl filled with 1-inch chunks of a good quality salami or other cured sausage, ready to spear and dip into the fondue. Allow about $1^{1}/_{2}$ to 2 pounds of sausage total.

Fresh Mushrooms

While most common crudités don't work with hot fondue, whole medium mushrooms are wonderfully dippable. Buy 1 or 2 pounds, wipe them clean with a damp cloth (*don't* wash them) and present them in a large earthenware bowl.

Pickled Cucumbers

Not strictly for dipping, pickles provide the perfect tangy contrast to the flavor of the fondue. Set out a bowl of your favorite spicy pickles or French cornichons.

Assorted Beers and Wines

Keep your selection of drinks as simple as the rest of the food—your favorite hearty beers and bottles of good, inexpensive red wine such as a nonvintage Burgundy and white wine such as Chablis.

Pacific Coast
Pizza Party

*T*iny, make-it-yourself pizzas with a rosemary crust are the centerpiece of this casual party inspired by the West Coast craze for designer versions of the traditional Italian favorite.

The only preparation you have to do is mix up a batch of dough a couple of hours or more before the party starts, make sauces (which you can also buy ready-made) and prepare the various topping ingredients.

The only special utensils you'll need are pizza bricks—ceramic slabs that give your oven a dry, radiant heat, promoting quick baking and crisp crusts. They're available at most cookware shops; buy the largest you can find and, if you have two ovens in your kitchen, get bricks for both, so you can have the maximum number of pizzas baking at once. A tapered wooden baking peel, for sliding pizzas in and out of the oven, helps, but you can also use a wide spatula or a rimless baking sheet.

Set out all the ingredients—dough, sauces and toppings—on your largest kitchen work surface, or on a table near the kitchen, leaving sufficient space for guests to prepare their pizzas. Demonstrate with one or two pizzas, encouraging guests to develop their own topping combinations. Then let them go to work, creating their own pizzas.

57

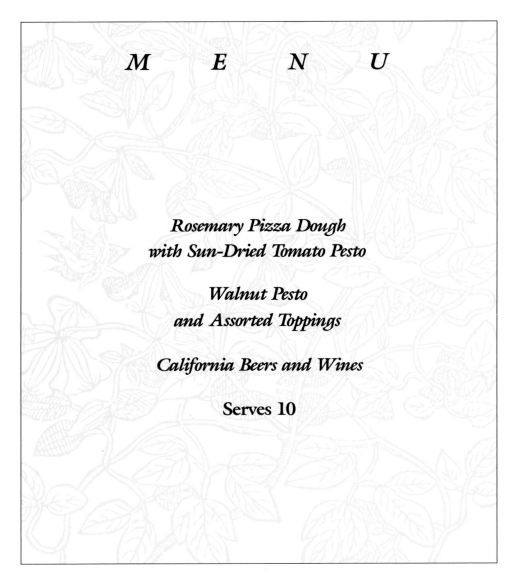

M E N U

Rosemary Pizza Dough with Sun-Dried Tomato Pesto

Walnut Pesto and Assorted Toppings

California Beers and Wines

Serves 10

Rosemary Pizza Dough

Dried rosemary gives this dough a wonderful aroma. You can start preparing the dough up to 1 hour before the party begins. It can also be made several hours ahead of time and left to rise more slowly in the refrigerator; or you can prepare it several days ahead and freeze it, defrosting the individual dough balls a couple of hours before the guests arrive.

Depending on your food processor, you may have to make this dough in 2 or more batches.

2 packets active dry yeast

1¹/₂ tablespoons sugar

6 cups all-purpose flour

6 tablespoons dried rosemary

1 tablespoon salt

6 tablespoons olive oil

Coarse semolina flour

In a bowl, dissolve the yeast and 2 teaspoons of the sugar in 1 cup of lukewarm water. Leave it until the yeast begins to foam, about 5 minutes.

Meanwhile, put the flour, rosemary, salt and remaining sugar in a food processor with the metal blade. Pulse several times to blend. With the machine running, pour in the yeast mixture and the oil;

then gradually pour in just enough water (about 2 cups), to form a smooth dough. Continue processing until the dough forms a ball that rides around the bowl on the blade.

Spray the inside of a large mixing bowl with nonstick spray or rub it with some olive oil. Put the dough in the bowl, cover it with a damp kitchen towel and leave it to rise at room temperature until doubled in bulk, 30 to 45 minutes. (If you're making the dough several hours in advance, it will rise more slowly in the refrigerator.)

Divide the risen dough into small balls weighing about 3 ounces each—about 30 balls in all. Roll them lightly in semolina flour and set aside. (To freeze them, wrap each ball securely in plastic wrap. Before preparing the pizzas, defrost the dough at room temperature for 2 hours or so, or 6 to 8 hours in the refrigerator.)

To make a pizza, put a pizza brick in the oven and preheat the oven to 550°. On a work surface lightly sprinkled with semolina, flatten a ball of dough by hand into a circle about 4 inches in diameter, pinching up a slightly raised rim. Spread about a tablespoon of sauce on top of the dough, then arrange your choice of toppings, finishing with an even sprinkling of cheese. With a peel, spatula or rimless baking sheet, slide the pizza onto the pizza brick. Bake for 8 to 10 minutes, until the crust is golden and the cheese is

melted and bubbly. Transfer the pizza from the oven to a serving plate; the pizza may be served whole, without cutting. (Warn guests to let the pizzas cool slightly before biting into them.)

Makes enough for about 30 4-inch hors d'oeuvre pizzas

Sun-Dried Tomato Pesto

This is an intensely flavored, and easily made, alternative to standard pizza sauce. You can make this several hours in advance.

1 1/2 cups drained oil-packed sun-dried tomatoes

3/4 cup olive oil (use the oil the tomatoes were packed in, if you like)

1/2 cup grated Parmesan cheese

6 tablespoons shelled pine nuts, toasted in a 450° oven until golden, 5 to 7 minutes

2 tablespoons chopped fresh parsley

2 tablespoons chopped fresh cilantro (or, if you don't like cilantro, the same amount more of parsley)

1 medium garlic clove

Place all the ingredients in a food processor fitted with the metal blade. Pulse the machine several times until the ingredients are coarsely chopped, then scrape

down the bowl. Process continuously until smooth; if the sauce seems too thick and pasty, pulse in a few tablespoons of hot water.

Store in the refrigerator, covered, until pizza preparation time.

Makes about 1 1/2 cups

Walnut Pesto

The walnuts are a rich-tasting twist on the classic Italian recipe. You can make this 1 hour in advance.

1 1/2 cups fresh basil leaves

3/4 cup olive oil

6 tablespoons grated Parmesan cheese

6 tablespoons shelled walnut pieces

2 medium garlic cloves

Place all the ingredients in a food processor fitted with the metal blade. Pulse the machine several times until the ingredients are coarsely chopped, then scrape down the bowl. Process continuously until smooth; if the sauce seems too thick and pasty, pulse in a few tablespoons of hot water.

Store in the refrigerator, covered, until it is time to make the pizzas.

Makes about 1 1/2 cups

Assorted Toppings

Inspire your guests with an array of toppings. Four or more selections that strike your fancy from each category will offer variety without overwhelming your guests. You can prepare these several hours in advance and store them in the refrigerator.

Meats, Poultry and Seafoods—For 10 guests, have on hand about 2 pounds total of meats, poultry and seafoods, divided according to your fancy and knowledge of your guests' tastes. Choose from among:

Pepperoni, thinly sliced

Prosciutto, thinly sliced and cut into 1/4-inch strips

Bresaola (air-cured beef), thinly sliced and cut into 1/4-inch strips

Fresh duck sausage, sliced 1/4 inch thick and briefly grilled

Cooked smoked chicken breast, cut into thin strips

Cooked smoked turkey breast, cut into thin strips

Cooked bay shrimp

Flaked cooked crabmeat

Anchovy fillets

Smoked clams or mussels

Vegetables—For 10 guests, offer about 2 pounds total of vegetable toppings, chosen from the following:

Domestic mushrooms, thinly sliced

Dried shiitake mushrooms, soaked in warm water until soft, stems trimmed off, caps cut into 1/4-inch-wide slices

Sun-dried tomatoes

Marinated black olives, pitted and halved

Marinated artichoke hearts, quartered

Red, green and yellow bell peppers, stemmed, seeded and cut into 1/4-inch strips

Canned green chiles, torn into thin strips

Asparagus tips, parboiled

Sweet Maui, Vidalia or Walla Walla onions, thinly sliced

Sweet red onions, thinly sliced

Cheeses—For 10 guests, set out about 1 cup of freshly grated Parmesan cheese to sprinkle over the sauce before adding other toppings. To melt on top of their pizzas, have on hand at least 1 pound of shredded mozzarella, plus another 1 to 1¹/₂ pounds of assorted cheeses, selected from the following:

Fresh, creamy goat cheese, coarsely crumbled for dotting on pizzas

Creamy garlic-herb cheese (such as Boursin™), for dotting on pizzas

Fontina, shredded into 1/2-inch pieces

Roquefort or other blue cheese, crumbled

Fresh mozzarella, sliced

Smoked mozzarella, shredded

Provolone, shredded

Monterey Jack, shredded

Some Suggested Combinations—
Most guests will leap at the chance to throw together their dream pizza from the ingredients you set out. But here are a few suggestions for those who can't make up their minds:

Sun-dried tomato pesto, shiitakes and duck sausage with mozzarella and Monterey Jack

Sun-dried tomato pesto, shrimp, black olives and fontina

Sun-dried tomato pesto, pepperoni and smoked mozzarella

Sun-dried tomato pesto and Roquefort cheese

Walnut pesto, smoked chicken, sweet onions and provolone

Walnut pesto, sun-dried tomatoes and goat cheese

Walnut pesto, crabmeat, garlic-herb cheese and mozzarella

© Guy Powers/Envision

California Beers and Wines

Have plenty of cold beer on hand, particularly some of the fine new beers coming out of the West, such as Anchor Steam, Sierra Nevada Pale Ale, and Henry Weinhard's Private Reserve. You also might want to offer a light, crisp Chardonnay and a California Zinfandel along with the requisite sparkling mineral water.

*Eastern
Seaboard
Elegance*

*S*eafood hors d'oeuvres are the foundation of this sophisticated buffet. There's something for every seafood lover: raw oysters and classic Oysters Rockefeller; succulent chilled shrimp; crisply browned crab cakes; and a smooth pâté of smoked trout. Make a formal evening of it, and serve the foods on your finest china, with your best silver, on a highly polished wooden table or sideboard. Or set the food out against a starched, white linen tablecloth. Candles set out in silver or crystal holders add just the right rich glow. Play the cool sounds of jazz fusion, or some big band era recordings. Your guests will feel as though they've been transported to a mansion in Newport.

Martinis—of course—are the drink of choice, though champagne or a good, flinty white wine such as a Fumé or Sauvignon Blanc would also be in order. Any elegant drink with a crisp, clean flavor that complements the seafood is perfect.

M E N U

Oysters on the Half Shell

Oysters Rockefeller

Jumbo Shrimp with Cocktail Sauce

Miniature Crab Cakes

Smoked Trout Pâté with Vegetables and Crackers

Martinis

Serves 10

Oysters on the Half Shell

30 oysters on the half shell

Crushed ice

1/4 cup finely chopped fresh shallots

5 lemons, quartered

10 thin slices brown bread, lightly buttered, cut into 3 fingers each

Most good suppliers can prepare the oysters for you on the half shell and pack them on crushed ice for you to carry home; however, you may have to bring your own containers. To open oysters yourself, use a special oyster knife with a sharp, short, sturdy blade. Holding the oyster in a folded kitchen towel to protect your hand from the knife, with the flat side of the shell up, carefully insert the blade between the shell halves and lever the shell open. Cut the oyster free from the top half and discard the top shell. Slide the knife under the bottom of the oyster to free it from the bottom shell, but leave it sitting there in its nectar.

And a note of caution: with pollution plaguing our seas, be sure to buy your oysters only from the most reputable purveyors. If the oysters look or smell at all suspicious, do *not* buy them. Be sure to keep the oysters well chilled, and don't open them more than an hour or so in advance.

Fill a large shallow serving tray with crushed ice, mounding the ice in the center. Put the shallots in a small bowl and set it into the center of the mound; place a small spoon in the bowl for guests to sprinkle shallots on their oysters, if they like. Set the raw oysters on the half shell into the ice. Arrange lemon wedges around the tray, for guests to squeeze over their oysters. Pass a separate plate of buttered brown bread.

Oysters Rockefeller

Start preparing the Oysters Rockefeller about 1 hour before the party begins, so they're ready to pop into the oven, in 2 or 3 batches if necessary, as guests arrive.

If your guests are certified oyster fanatics, increase the quantities below.

30 oysters on the half shell

1/2 cup unsalted butter

3 strips lean bacon, cut crosswise into 1/4-inch pieces

1 small onion, finely chopped

1 medium garlic clove, finely chopped

1 ten-ounce package frozen spinach, defrosted

1/2 cup heavy cream

10 tablespoons grated Parmesan cheese

10 tablespoons fine, dry bread crumbs

1/4 teaspoon cayenne

Salt

Remove the oysters from the half shells, draining and saving the oyster liquor from the shells and setting the shells aside. (See, Oysters on the Half Shell.)

Preheat the oven to 450°.

Melt 3 tablespoons of the butter in a medium saucepan over medium heat. Add the bacon, onion and garlic and sauté until the onion and garlic are transparent, 3 to 5 minutes. Add the oyster liquor, spinach, cream, half the Parmesan cheese, half the bread crumbs and the cayenne. Cook, stirring until the mixture is thick and creamy, 5 to 10 minutes. Season to taste with salt.

In a separate saucepan, melt the remaining butter. In a bowl, stir together the melted butter and the remaining Parmesan and bread crumbs.

Distribute the spinach mixture among the oyster shells. Set an oyster on top of the spinach in each shell and top it with some of the other mixture.

Fill a shallow oven-to-table baking dish with rock salt and set into the salt bed as many Oysters Rockefeller as will fit. Bake for 20 to 25 minutes, then serve immediately, placing the baking dish on the serving table.

Makes 30 hors d'oeuvres

© FPG International

Jumbo Shrimp with Cocktail Sauce

This is the classic hors d'oeuvre shrimp presentation.

You can cook the shrimp and prepare the sauce several hours in advance, keeping both covered in the refrigerator, airtight, until serving.

40 extra-large shrimp (about 3¹/₄ pounds total)

3/4 cup tomato ketchup

2 tablespoons grated horseradish

2 tablespoons lemon juice

2 teaspoons lime juice

3 drops Tabasco™ sauce

Bring a large pot of water to a boil and cook the shrimp, in batches if necessary, until they turn bright pink, 3 to 4 minutes. Drain well, then rinse under cold running water until cool. Carefully peel the shrimp, leaving their tails on. With a small, sharp knife, make a shallow incision along the outer curves and devein them. Refrigerate, covered.

In a bowl, stir together the remaining ingredients. Cover and refrigerate.
To serve, fill a shallow serving tray with crushed ice, mounding the ice in the center. Put the cocktail sauce in a small bowl set into the center of the mound, for dipping the shrimp. Arrange the shrimp around the bowl on top of the crushed ice.

Makes 40 hors d'oeuvres

Miniature Crab Cakes

A sophisticated version of an old Eastern Seaboard favorite. Make the mixture up to several hours in advance, form it into little cakes and refrigerate it. Then fry the crab cakes in several batches as guests arrive.

1¹/₄ pounds cooked crabmeat, flaked and picked clean of shell and cartilage

1 egg, well beaten

3/4 cup mayonnaise

1/2 cup fine fresh bread crumbs

1/4 cup finely chopped fresh parsley

3 tablespoons finely chopped fresh chives

1 tablespoon fresh lemon juice

1/2 teaspoon salt

1/2 teaspoon paprika

1/4 cup all-purpose flour

1/4 cup unsalted butter

1/4 cup vegetable oil

3 lemons, quartered

In a mixing bowl, stir together the crabmeat, egg, mayonnaise, bread crumbs, parsley, chives, lemon juice, salt and paprika until thoroughly blended.

A generous tablespoon at a time, shape the mixture into small, round patties about 1/2 inch thick. Place them on a tray lined with wax paper; cover with more wax paper and refrigerate.

To cook the crab cakes, lightly dust them on both sides with flour. Melt the butter with the oil in a large skillet over medium heat. Fry the crab cakes in several batches until deep golden brown, 3 to 5 minutes on each side. Drain on paper towels and serve hot, accompanied by lemon wedges.

Makes about 40 crab cakes

Smoked Trout Pâté

The distinctive, elegant taste of smoked trout shines through beautifully in this simply made spread. Prepare the pâté and chill it in molds at least three hours in advance.

3/4 pound smoked trout, skinned, filleted and flaked

3/4 cup heavy cream

2 tablespoons grated horseradish

1 tablespoon lemon juice

1/4 teaspoon salt

1/4 teaspoon freshly ground white pepper

1/2 cup drained low-fat ricotta cheese

1/4 cup finely chopped fresh chives

Fresh parsley sprigs, for garnish

Assorted vegetables and crackers

Put the trout in a food processor and pulse several times, scraping down the bowl, until finely chopped. Add the cream, horseradish, lemon juice, salt and pepper and process until smooth. Then add the ricotta and continue processing until smoothly blended. Briefly pulse in the chives.

Pack the mixture into a serving crock or into a lightly oiled decorative mold and chill, covered, in the refrigerator. To serve, place the crock—or unmold the

mold—in the center of a serving platter. Garnish the mousse with parsley and set a pair of spreading knives alongside it. Fill the tray with assorted fresh vegetables—sliced cucumber or jicama, wide carrot sticks, celery stalks and so on—as well as water biscuits or other good crackers on which to spread the pâté.

Makes about 2 1/2 cups

Martinis

This cocktail is back in vogue. Serve it in the classic, 6-ounce V-shaped martini glass.

Part of the thrill of a good martini is its iciness. To achieve the right effect, keep your gin bottles in the freezer, and put the glasses in the freezer at least 30 minutes in advance, removing them just before you pour the drinks.

Mix the martinis in several batches, depending on the size of your cocktail shaker and how many takers you have at any moment. Count on at least 1 martini per guest.

1/4 cup vermouth

2 1/2 cups ice-cold gin

8 jumbo pimiento-stuffed olives, drained

4 cocktail sticks or toothpicks

Fill a cocktail shaker with ice cubes. Pour the vermouth over the ice and, with a strainer over the shaker, pour off and discard *all* of the vermouth, leaving just what coats the ice.

Pour the gin into the shaker, cover and immediately shake vigorously for at least 10 seconds. Immediately strain the liquid into chilled martini glasses. Spear two olives on each cocktail stick, put one stick in each glass and serve at once.

Makes 4 five-ounce drinks

Italian
Antipasto
Table

*T*he antipasto *table is one of the great glories of dining out in
Italy. In fine restaurants, whatever the prices, this array of small
dishes served before (anti) the main repast (pasto) is beautifully
displayed on a table near the entrance or at the center of the
restaurant—there to catch the eye and whet the appetite of every guest
who passes by. Fresh and marinated vegetables; cooked and cured
seafoods; sliced sausages, hams and cheeses: the selection is stunning in
its variety and bounty.*

*What makes an antipasto party so easy to throw in your own home is
the range of prepared products available in any well-stocked Italian deli
or gourmet market. Several of the items in the following menu require
only decorative arrangement on a platter before serving. Others are
easily prepared in advance.*

*Set out the antipasto on rustic pottery—Italian faience would be a
perfect choice, although anything plain and heavy will do nicely. Have
small plates and forks on hand. Add a vase of robust flowers—anemones,
lilies, poppies, peonies, gerberas and the like.*

73

M E N U

Roma Tomatoes with Buffalo Mozzarella and Pesto

Grilled Zucchini and Eggplant

Marinated Peppers

Assorted Olives

Tonno e Fagioli

Bagna Cauda with Fresh Vegetables

Assorted Italian Cold Cuts and Cheeses

Assorted Italian Bread Sticks and Breads

Drinks: Italian White and Red Wines, Campari and Soda, Italian Mineral Water

Serves 12

Roma Tomatoes with Buffalo Mozzarella and Pesto

Small, egg-shaped Roma tomatoes are the perfect size for these. Make sure to buy firm tomatoes that will slice well and hold their shape.

Fresh buffalo mozzarella can be found in many good delis nowadays. If it is unavailable, substitute the best packaged mozzarella you can find.

This dish is quickly assembled, and should be prepared no more than a half hour or so before the party begins.

1/3 cup pine nuts

1 1/2 cups fresh basil leaves

1/3 cup grated Parmesan cheese

1/2 cup olive oil

3 medium garlic cloves, peeled

1 pound fresh buffalo mozzarella cheese

10 medium firm Roma tomatoes

Preheat the oven to 450°. Toast the pine nuts 5 to 7 minutes, or until golden. Let them cool. Place the toasted pine nuts, basil, Parmesan, olive oil and garlic cloves in a food processor fitted with the metal blade. Pulse the machine a few times to chop the ingredients coarsely; scrape down the bowl, then process continuously until the pesto sauce is smooth.

Drain the mozzarella if necessary and pat it dry with paper towels. With a small, sharp knife, slice and cut the mozzarella into 40 pieces, each about 1/4 to 1/3 inch thick; the exact size and shape of the pieces will depend on the shape and density of the particular cheese.

Trim both ends of each tomato; then slice each tomato crosswise into 4 equal pieces and place the slices on a serving platter. Generously spread the top of each slice with the pesto sauce, then top with a piece of mozzarella.

Makes 40 hors d'oeuvres

Grilled Zucchini and Eggplant

Start marinating the vegetables 1½ hours or more before guests arrive. Once grilled, they can be arranged on their serving platter and left at room temperature.

1¹/₂ pounds medium zucchini, trimmed, cut lengthwise into 1/4-inch-thick slices

1¹/₂ pounds eggplant, trimmed, cut lengthwise into 1/4-inch-thick slices

1¹/₂ cups olive oil

3 tablespoons lemon juice

1 tablespoon dried oregano

Salt and freshly ground white pepper

In a large mixing bowl, gently toss the zucchini and eggplant slices with the olive oil, lemon juice and oregano. Marinate at room temperature for 1 hour, occasionally stirring gently.

Preheat the grill or broiler until very hot.

In batches, lightly sprinkle the zucchini and eggplant slices with salt and white pepper and grill or broil about 1 minute per side, until golden. As they're done, arrange them decoratively on a large platter. Brush them lightly with any remaining marinade. Serve lukewarm or at room temperature.

Serves 12

Marinated Peppers

Red bell peppers are most authentic here, but you can certainly vary the dish by substituting green or yellow peppers. Prepare them the night before, if you like. The peppers taste better the longer they are marinated.

6 medium-to-large red bell peppers

3/4 cup olive oil

1/4 cup balsamic vinegar

1 teaspoon dried oregano

1/2 teaspoon dried thyme

1/2 teaspoon dried rosemary

Preheat the oven to 500°. Put the peppers on a baking sheet lined with aluminum foil and roast them in the oven about 25 minutes, turning them 2 or 3 times so they roast evenly, until their skins are evenly blistered and blackened. Remove them from the oven and leave them covered with a kitchen towel until they are cool enough to handle.

With your fingers, pull out and discard the stems. Peel away the blackened skins. Tear open the peppers and remove the seeds and white ribs inside, using a teaspoon to gather up the seeds if necessary.

Tear each pepper into about 6 equal pieces. In a nonreactive bowl, toss the peppers with the olive oil, vinegar and herbs. Cover them with plastic wrap and marinate for at least 3 hours, or preferably, overnight.

Serves 12

Assorted Olives

Many delis—Italian and others—now carry a good selection of marinated, unpitted olives: black and green; large and small; in brine and in oil; with and without herbs. Taste several and buy at least two different kinds to add to your antipasto buffet. While size and weight will vary, you should get enough to allow at least three of each kind for each guest— roughly a cup of each kind of olive.

Tonno e Fagioli

This favorite Tuscan combination of white beans and chunky canned tuna takes almost no time to prepare. The beans may be assembled and dressed two hours ahead of serving; top with the tuna, scallions, parsley and pepper just before serving. Be sure to leave the tuna in large, bite-size chunks.

1/2 cup olive oil

2 tablespoons lemon juice

3 medium garlic cloves, finely chopped

3 cans cannellini (white kidney beans), rinsed and thoroughly drained

Salt

2 cans tuna in olive oil

3 medium scallions, finely sliced

2 tablespoons coarsely chopped fresh parsley, preferably Italian

Freshly ground black pepper

In a mixing bowl, stir together the oil, lemon juice and garlic. Pour this dressing over the beans and toss gently but thoroughly; season to taste with salt. Arrange in a shallow serving dish.

Break the tuna in large chunks, scattering it evenly over the beans. Garnish with scallions and parsley and a generous grinding of black pepper.

Bagna Cauda with Fresh Vegetables

You can almost make a meal out of this traditional Piedmontese dip, a "hot bath" of white-truffle-scented olive oil, butter, cream, anchovies and garlic. Whip it up just before guests arrive and present it in a fondue pot set in the middle of a large tray filled with bite-size seasonal vegetables for dipping—broccoli, cauliflower, fennel, radishes, celery, mushrooms—and alongside a basket of Italian bread sticks and fingers of Italian sourdough bread.

Most gourmet and Italian delis now carry white truffle olive oil. Though costly, it is far less expensive than buying fresh white truffles to add to the dip.

3 cups heavy cream

3 tablespoons unsalted butter

3 tablespoons white-truffle-scented olive oil

6 medium garlic cloves, very finely chopped

3 two-ounce tins anchovy fillets, drained and finely chopped

12 cups assorted fresh vegetables, cut into bite-size chunks

Italian bread sticks and sourdough bread

In a heavy saucepan, simmer the cream over medium heat, stirring frequently, until it reduces by half.

In a separate saucepan over low heat, melt the butter with the oil. Add the garlic and anchovies and stir until the garlic is soft and the anchovies dissolve. Raise the heat slightly and, with a wire whisk, slowly stir in the cream until the sauce is smoothly blended.

Transfer the sauce to a fondue pot or heat-proof casserole over a spirit flame. Place it on a large serving platter, surrounded by vegetables and bread for dipping.

Assorted Italian Cold Cuts and Cheeses

There are so many cold cuts to choose from in a good Italian deli: wonderfully intense, air-cured prosciutto; subtly spicy mortadella sausage; hard, rich and meaty salamis; and on and on. Sample and select a few that suit your fancy, allowing 2 to 3 ounces total of cold cuts per person. Have them sliced thin—make the prosciutto paper thin. Then arrange them attractively on a large platter, leaving those sausages with smaller diameters flat and rolling up the larger slices.

Intersperse thin, rolled slices of provolone and smoked mozzarella cheese among the sausages, allowing a total of about 2 ounces of cheese per person. For an extra-special touch, buy a 1/2-to-3/4-pound block of a not-too-dry Parmesan cheese and, with a shaver-type cheese slicer, cut decorative curls of Parmesan to scatter about the platter.

Assorted Italian Breads and Breadsticks

Seek out a bakery and buy a good selection of different breads—whichever are best, freshest, and most capture your fancy—to accompany your buffet. Set them out on a wooden carving board with a good, sturdy bread knife, and let your guests slice for themselves. Pile rolls in a napkin-lined basket or pottery bowl.

While you're at it, it would also be worthwhile to pick up some packaged Italian breadsticks—the thin kind known as *grissini*—at your Italian deli. These are incomparably crisp and delicious, eaten plain or used for dipping.

A Note on Beverages

Stick to the basics: a good, drinkable red such as a Chianti, Bardolino or Valpolicella; a light, clean white such as Verdicchio or Soave. For guests who'd like a cocktail, have a bottle or two of Campari on hand to mix with club soda and ice—in equal proportions or two parts Campari to one of soda, depending on how each guest feels about the refreshingly bitter herbal taste of Campari; have orange slices on hand to garnish each glass. And for guests who are avoiding alcohol, have *aqua minerale* on hand; San Pellegrino is a widely available Italian brand that has fine bubbles and a clean, clear flavor.

© Burke/Triolo

77

Middle
Eastern Feast

*T*hroughout the Middle East—from Greece and Turkey to Lebanon, Israel and the Arab states—guests are welcomed lavishly with an array of traditional dishes such as those in this menu. Though precise customs may differ from country to country along with recipe names and slight variations, the ingredients and preparations remain basically the same—rich, earthy spreads of ground chick peas and roasted eggplant; trays of tangy olives and goat cheese; and fragrant dishes of ground lamb.

Almost everything for this menu is easily purchased in a well-stocked supermarket—though you may have to look in the foreign foods section or seek out a Middle Eastern market for the tahini (sesame paste) and tarama (carp roe).

Set your table with a richly embroidered cloth or tapestry, or a deep red or rich brown tablecloth. Serve the food on earthenware or plain white dishes and platters, accented with any brass, copper or other metal trays, bowls or table accessories you have. Choose opulent flowers in deep, lush colors—roses, anemones and dahlias, for example. And set the mood with Greek bouzouki music or recordings of Israeli or Arabic folk tunes.

81

M E N U

Hummus

Baba Ganoosh

Taramasalata

Pita Bread

*Platter of Feta Cheese, Greek Olives,
Tomatoes and Scallions*

Tabbouleh on Baby Lettuce Leaves

Grape Leaves Stuffed with Rice, Pine Nuts and Dill

Spinach and Feta Filled Phyllo Triangles

Fried Kibbeh Balls

Middle Eastern Drinks

Serves 12

Hummus

This spread of ground garbanzo beans gains a seductively rich character from *tahini*, sesame paste. You can find the paste in cans or jars in the imported food section of most supermarkets. And don't bother cooking the garbanzos from scratch; the cooked canned ones work just fine.

The hummus can be made several hours in advance, or even the night before.

2 fifteen-and-a-half ounce cans garbanzo beans, drained

6 medium garlic cloves

2/3 cup tahini

1/2 cup lemon juice

2 tablespoons olive oil

Salt and freshly ground white pepper

Chopped fresh parsley leaves

Place the garbanzos, garlic, tahini, lemon juice and olive oil in a food processor fitted with the metal blade and process until smoothly pureed. Season to taste with salt and white pepper, pulsing and retasting as necessary. Cover and refrigerate.

About 30 minutes before serving, spread the hummus in a shallow serving bowl and garnish liberally with a pattern of fresh parsley leaves. Put a serving spoon alongside so guests can scoop the hummus onto their plates. Have a basket of pita bread wedges nearby for dipping.

Makes about 4 cups

Baba Ganoosh

The name means harem girl—perhaps because the texture of this roasted eggplant dip is so voluptuous. Make the dip several hours ahead of time or the night before the party.

1 1/2 pounds eggplant

3 medium garlic cloves

1/3 cup lemon juice

1/4 cup tahini

3 tablespoons olive oil

Salt and freshly ground white pepper

3 medium scallions, thinly sliced crosswise

2 tablespoons chopped fresh mint leaves

Preheat the broiler until very hot. With a fork or skewer, prick the skin of the eggplant several times. Broil the eggplant about 4 inches from the heat, turning occasionally, for about 20 minutes, until the skin is charred evenly. Let the eggplant cool. Then peel away the charred exterior.

Put the eggplant flesh in a food processor with the metal blade and add the garlic, lemon juice, tahini, and half the oil. Process until smoothly pureed. Season to taste with salt and white pepper, pulsing and retasting as necessary. Pulse in the scallions. Cover and refrigerate.

Before serving, spread the puree smoothly in a shallow bowl. Then, with the edge of a spoon, make a shallow crisscross pattern on its surface. Drizzle the remaining oil over it and sprinkle it with the mint. Put a serving spoon alongside the baba ganoosh so guests can scoop the spread onto their plates. Accompany it with a basket of pita bread wedges for dipping.

Makes about 3 cups

Taramasalata

To my taste, this is the best of all Middle Eastern dips. Literally "carp roe salad," it's a blend of pink, salted carp roe, bread, olive oil, lemon juice, onion and garlic. If you can't find tarama in your market's imported foods section and don't have a Middle Eastern shop nearby, substitute the more readily available salmon roe, which will give a similar color to the dish and will be just as delicious.

1 1/2 cups packed crustless sourdough bread

1 cup milk

1/2 small sweet onion

1 garlic clove

3/4 cup tarama or salmon roe

6 tablespoons fresh lemon juice

1 1/4 cups olive oil

Salt and freshly ground white pepper

2 medium scallions, sliced thinly crosswise

In a bowl, soak the bread in the milk for a few minutes.

Meanwhile, place the onion and garlic in a food processor fitted with the metal blade and pulse until finely chopped. Squeeze as much of the milk as possible from the bread; discard the milk and add the bread to the processor. Process until the bread is smoothly pureed.

Add the tarama and process until smooth, then process in the lemon juice. With the machine running, add the oil in a thin, steady stream, stopping when the taramasalata is as thick and as smooth as a mayonnaise. Season to taste with salt and white pepper.

Refrigerate the taramasalata, covered, until you are ready to serve it. Spread it smoothly in a shallow bowl and garnish it with scallions.

Makes about 3 cups

Pita Bread

The Middle Eastern specialty known as pita bread—and sometimes as pocket bread—is now a common sight in supermarkets. You'll often find variations on the white-bread variety—including whole-wheat and sesame-seed pitas. Buy a good selection, allowing at least one pita per person.

For buffets, keep a steady supply of fresh pitas at the table; don't put them all out at once, or latecomers won't be able to enjoy them at their best. Heat the pitas for a few minutes in a 400° oven, or pop them under a hot broiler until they begin to brown slightly and crisp up. Then cut them into narrow wedges; or cut them in half, then crosswise into fingers about an inch wide and pile them into a napkin-lined basket or bowl.

Platter of Feta Cheese, Tomatoes, Greek Olives and Scallions

Set out a large tray, or several smaller dishes or trays placed side by side, filled with these typical Middle Eastern country pleasures.

Feta is a creamy, firm and crumbly goat's milk cheese, with a tangy flavor and pronounced saltiness. Allow about 2 ounces of feta per person. Cut or break the feta into rough chunks about 3/4 to 1 inch across.

Most delis carry some sort of marinated Greek olive. Sample a few, along with any other black olives that strike your fancy. Buy about 3 dozen of the olives that taste best to you, bearing in mind that they should have sufficient tang to stand up to the feta and the other dishes you're serving.

Buy the firmest, ripest, crispest tomatoes you can find and cut them into wedges that can be polished off in 2 bites or less, allowing 2 or 3 wedges per person. And buy about 2 dozen small to medium scallions, trimming their roots and the top inch or so of their greens.

Arrange the platter up to 1 hour in advance and refrigerate, covered, until serving time.

Tabbouleh on Baby Lettuce Leaves

Popular throughout the Middle East, this light, aromatic salad is based on bulgur-dried cracked wheat. You may make it 2 to 3 hours ahead of time.

1 cup bulgur wheat

3/4 cup finely chopped fresh parsley

3/4 cup finely chopped scallions

1/2 cup finely chopped fresh mint

3 medium tomatoes, cored, seeded and finely chopped

1/4 cup olive oil

1/4 cup lemon juice

1 medium garlic clove, finely chopped

Salt and freshly ground white pepper

Baby romaine and Bibb lettuce leaves

Put the bulgur in a bowl and add enough cold water to cover it. Soak for 10 minutes. Then drain away the water, picking up handfuls of the grain and squeezing out the water.

Put the bulgur in a mixing bowl and toss it well with the parsley, scallions, mint and tomatoes. Stir together the oil, lemon juice and garlic and toss the bulgur mixture with this dressing. Season to taste and refrigerate, covered.

Mound the tabbouleh in the middle of a large, round platter, surrounded by baby lettuce leaves. Spoon some into the center of a few leaves to show guests how to eat it.

Makes about 4 cups

Grape Leaves Stuffed with Rice, Pine Nuts and Dill

You can find jars or vacuum-packed pouches of grapevine leaves pickled in brine, which are perfect for this recipe.

Prepare the stuffed grape leaves as much as 2 days in advance, keeping them in the refrigerator.

© Ricardo Marcialis/Photo Researchers

6 tablespoons olive oil

1 medium onion, finely chopped

2 cups water

1 cup long-grain rice

1 teaspoon salt

1/4 teaspoon black pepper

1/2 cup pine nuts

1/4 cup chopped fresh dill

2 tablespoons grated lemon zest

Heat half the oil in a medium saucepan over medium heat. Add the onion and sauté 3 to 5 minutes until it turns transparent. Add the water and bring it to a boil. Add the rice, salt and pepper, reduce the heat to a bare simmer, cover the pan and cook about 20 minutes, until the rice is tender and all the water has been absorbed.

Meanwhile, heat the remaining oil in a small skillet over medium heat. Add the pine nuts and sauté them 2 to 3 minutes until light golden brown. Remove the skillet from the heat and set them aside in the oil.

In a mixing bowl, stir together the rice, pine nuts with their oil, dill and lemon zest. Set the mixture aside.

Cover the bottom of a 3-quart covered casserole with 10 of the grape leaves, laying them flat and overlapping them. Then, one at a time, stuff 40 of the remaining leaves: place a leaf shiny side down on a work surface; place a generous tablespoon of the rice mixture in its center; fold the stem end over the stuffing, fold in the sides, then roll the leaf up toward its tip to make a neat cylinder. As each roll is finished, place it flap-down in the casserole, stacking the leaves in neat layers. Cover the top layer with the remaining leaves.

Pour 1/4 cup of cold water into the casserole, then place a heatproof plate upside down on top of the leaves. Cover the casserole and cook the leaves over low heat for about 45 minutes.

Uncover the casserole, carefully remove the plate, and let the grape leaves cool to room temperature. Then refrigerate them, covered, until it's time to serve them. Carefully remove the stuffed leaves, stacking them on a serving platter.

Makes about 40 hors d'oeuvres

Spinach and Feta Phyllo Triangles

Phyllo—wafer-thin sheets of Middle Eastern pastry—provides the crisp, light casing for this savory hors d'oeuvre filling. Packaged phyllo is widely available, usually in the frozen foods section of the supermarket; let it thaw in the refrigerator for 24 hours before using it.

You can prepare the pastries up to 2 days in advance and refrigerate them so they're ready to bake just before guests start arriving. Divide them into 2 or 3 batches, so they can be enjoyed while still hot from the oven.

1 pound spinach, stemmed and thoroughly washed.

1/2 pound feta cheese, drained and crumbled

1/2 pound ricotta cheese, well drained

2 eggs, well beaten

1/2 medium onion, finely chopped

1/4 teaspoon freshly ground white pepper

1 small pinch nutmeg

8 (16-by-18-inch) sheets phyllo

1 stick unsalted butter, melted

Bring a pot of water to a boil. Add the spinach, stir and immediately drain. Rinse the spinach briefly under cold running water; then, with your hands, squeeze the spinach as hard as possible to rid it of water. Chop the spinach coarsely.

Put the chopped spinach in a bowl with the feta, ricotta, eggs, onions, pepper and nutmeg; stir until well mixed.

Stack the sheets of phyllo on a work surface and, with sharp scissors, carefully cut the stack to make 6 strips, 3 inches wide and 16 inches long.

To shape a triangle, take a strip of phyllo and place 1 tablespoon of the filling at the end of the strip nearest you. Fold the left-hand corner of the strip diagonally over the filling so the narrow edge meets the right-hand side. Fold the triangle that now encloses the filling upwards so its right edge lines up with the strip of dough. Continue folding the phyllo up to the top of the strip, tucking the top edge into the nearest fold.

Continue with the remaining phyllo strips and filling.

If you like, refrigerate the triangles at this stage on a covered tray.

Preheat the oven to 350°. Brush a baking sheet generously with butter. Place the phyllo triangles on the sheet and brush their tops with more butter. Bake them until they are golden, 25 to 30 minutes. Carefully transfer them to a serving platter.

Makes about 4 dozen triangles

Fried Kibbeh Balls

Mixtures of ground lamb, bulgur and mint are popular throughout the Middle East—eaten raw, baked in casseroles, or, as here, fried as wonderfully aromatic meatballs.

Make the lamb mixture several hours ahead of time, shape it into balls and set them aside on a covered plate. Then fry them up fresh and hot as guests arrive.

3/4 cup bulgur

1 pound lean ground lamb

1 egg, lightly beaten

1 medium onion, finely chopped

1/2 cup finely chopped fresh mint

1/4 cup finely chopped fresh parsley

1/2 teaspoon ground cumin

1/4 teaspoon salt

1/4 teaspoon freshly ground black pepper

Put the bulgur in a bowl and add enough cold water to cover. Soak for 10 minutes. Then drain away the water, picking up handfuls of the grain and squeezing it out.

In a mixing bowl, stir together the bulgur, lamb, egg, onion, mint, parsley, cumin, salt and pepper until thoroughly blended.

Wetting your hands to keep the mixture from sticking, form it into tablespoon-size balls. Place them on a platter lightly coated with olive oil. Cover them with plastic wrap and refrigerate until serving time.

In a heavy skillet, heat a few tablespoons of olive oil over medium-high heat. Add the kibbeh balls in several batches, without overcrowding, and fry them until evenly browned, about 5 minutes. Drain on paper towels and serve on a napkin-lined platter, toothpicks optional.

Makes about 4 dozen balls

Middle Eastern Drinks

Offer your guests a selection of different typical Middle Eastern drinks with the hors d'oeuvres.

Wine is certainly appropriate. If you're turned off by the resinous taste of Greek *retsina*, opt for the widely available Demestica, red or white, an eminently drinkable nonresinated wine. Turkey, too, produces some good wines, though you don't see many in the West; ask your wine merchant. And don't shun Israeli wines, which get a bad rap because of the sickly sweet ceremonial varieties. Israeli vintners have made great strides in recent years, and you may find a few surprises in your wine shop; a good fallback are the quite drinkable wines of the Carmel label.

Beer, though less traditional in the region, is a refreshing companion to the strong flavors of the food. Though you may find stray Middle Eastern labels, your best bet is to go for your favorite light lager.

For adventurous guests, have a bottle of the popular Middle Eastern anise-flavored aperitif called *arak, raki* or, in Greece, *ouzo*. Mixed with cold water or served on the rocks, the clear liquid turns a milky white, and its slightly sweet, aromatic taste provides an interesting counterpoint to the buffet.

Have some softer options on hand, too. Fruit juices and punches, particularly lemonade, are popular Middle Eastern quaffs.

© FPG International/Peter Johansky

Asian Medley

Recently, our understanding of Asian cuisine has extended far beyond the familiar dishes of China and Japan. Innovative Western chefs—particularly those working in California, the American side of the Pacific Rim—are creating a new pan-Asian cuisine that embraces Chinese, Japanese, Thai, Indian, Korean, Indonesian, Vietnamese and other Asian cooking.

All these Asian cuisines have their typical hors d'oeuvre dishes, and the following menu showcases a number of them together. Asian markets are widespread today, and they'll carry the few specialty foods you'll need; it's likely that you'll also find them in the foreign foods section of a well-stocked supermarket.

Many Asian markets also carry inexpensive dishware—simple geometric shapes in plain white or traditional patterned finishes—that you can use for displaying the buffet. Or just set out your plainest china platters or other basic tableware that will show off the hors d'oeuvres nicely. In addition to hors d'oeuvre forks, set out chopsticks—fancy lacquered or disposable wooden pairs.

To complete the mood, have a selection of Asian sounds—from Ravi Shankar records to Indonesian folk music to the New Age sounds of Kitaro.

$M \quad E \quad N \quad U$

Shrimp Sushi

Indonesian Shrimp Chips

Steamed Scallop Shiu Mai with Spicy Soy Dip

Assorted Asian Pickles

Vietnamese Chicken Spring Rolls with Nuoc Cham Sauce

Lamb Tikka Sticks with Mint Raita

Hot Indonesian Peanut Dip with Fresh Vegetables

Hot Sake and Assorted Asian Beers

Serves 12

Shrimp Sushi

Not *all* sushi is raw fish, and this version of the Japanese specialty showcases large, cooked shrimp.

Use only short-grained, unconverted rice, and cook it several hours before the party. The sushi are easily assembled an hour or two in advance and kept cold in the refrigerator until guests arrive.

2 cups short-grain rice, rinsed thoroughly under cold running water, then drained well

1 (2¹/₂-inch) square kombu (Japanese dried kelp), rinsed thoroughly under cold running water

2¹/₄ cups cold water

1 cup plus 1 tablespoon rice vinegar

2 tablespoons sugar

2 teaspoons salt

48 raw medium shrimp (about 3 pounds total)

Wasabi paste, or powdered wasabi mixed with a little warm water to make a spreadable paste

Soy sauce

To make the sushi rice, put the rinsed and drained rice in a medium nonreactive saucepan. Bury the kombu in the rice and add the cold water. Let the rice soak for about 30 minutes, then bring it to a boil over high heat. Remove and discard the kombu, cover the pan, reduce the heat to medium, and cook the rice until it has absorbed all the water, about 10 minutes. Reduce the heat as low as possible and cook 5 minutes more, then remove the pan from the heat and leave the pan covered for an additional 5 minutes.

While the rice is cooking, in a separate, small, nonreactive pan, bring the vinegar, sugar and salt to a boil, stirring to dissolve the sugar and salt. Remove from the heat.

When the rice is done cooking, empty it onto a large, shallow platter. While turning it over lightly, back and forth, with a plastic or wooden spatula, sprinkle it evenly with the vinegar mixture until thoroughly mixed. Leave the rice to cool to room temperature, and use it within several hours.

Run a long wooden toothpick under the shell between the legs of each shrimp, to keep them straight as they cook. Bring a large pot of water to a boil and cook the shrimp, in batches if necessary, about 3 minutes, until they turn bright pink. Drain and rinse under cold running water until cool.

Remove the toothpicks and carefully peel the shrimp, leaving their tails on. With a small, sharp knife, make a shallow incision along the back of each shrimp and devein it. Then carefully cut it along the inner curve to butterfly it flat.

Moisten your palm with a little water and place about 2 tablespoons of sushi rice in it, and shape the rice to make a neat oblong slightly shorter than a shrimp. Lightly smear one side of the rice with wasabi (this horseradish paste is very spicy, so you might want to make some of the pieces without wasabi). Then gently press a shrimp, butterflied side down, on top. Place the sushi on a serving tray. Repeat these steps with the remaining rice and shrimp, leaving space in the center of the tray for a small bowl. Cover the tray of shrimp sushi with plastic wrap and refrigerate it until serving time. Then fill the bowl with soy sauce for dipping, and serve.

Makes 4 dozen hors d'oeuvres

Indonesian Shrimp Chips

These are to Indonesia what potato chips are to the West. Look for the packaged, ready-to-fry chips—often labeled *krupuk*—in the Asian food section.

Fry them in the hot vegetable oil (you use the same oil you fry the Vietnamese Spring Rolls in). Add a small handful of the chips to the oil; they'll puff up several times their size instantly. The moment they're puffed, remove them from the oil with a wire skimmer and drain them on paper towels. Then transfer them to a napkin-lined basket. Keep fresh batches coming throughout the party.

© Riccardo Marcialis/Photo Researchers

93

Steamed Scallop Shiu Mai

Virtually any Asian market, and most good cookware shops, will sell you Chinese bamboo steamer baskets, which are not only the best utensil for cooking these dumplings, but are also the best tray for serving them. Buy at least two large baskets. Arrange some assembled shiu mai in one, steam them, then carry the basket to the serving table, placing it on a large platter to catch any drips. Get the next basket going while your guests are eating the first batch.

Shop for 3-inch-diameter round shiu mai wrappers, which are often sold commercially packaged in airtight containers. If you can't find them, substitute the more readily available square wonton skins, which are the same basic dough, and cut them into the desired shape with a round cookie cutter.

The dumplings themselves are easily assembled a few hours in advance.

1 pound baby bay scallops, rinsed and patted dry

1/2 cup drained water chestnuts

1 1/2 tablespoons finely chopped fresh ginger

2 tablespoons cornstarch

1 1/2 tablespoons sea salt

1 tablespoon Chinese rice wine or dry sherry

1/2 teaspoon freshly ground white pepper

3 egg whites

1 bunch fresh cilantro

2 medium scallions, thinly sliced

48 shiu mai wrappers

Peanut or sesame oil

Place 3/4 pound of the scallops in a food processor fitted with the metal blade. Add the water chestnuts and ginger and pulse the machine until coarsely chopped. Sprinkle in the cornstarch, salt, rice wine and pepper evenly and add the egg whites. Process until smooth, stopping once or twice to scrape down the bowl.

Separate out 48 single leaves of cilantro and set them aside. Measure enough of the remaining leaves to make a loose 1/2 cup and add them to the processor with the scallions and remaining scallops. Pulse the machine several times to combine them with the scallop purée, leaving small chunks of scallop in the mixture.

Holding a wrapper in your hand, place a heaping teaspoonful of the filling in the center, then gently squeeze the wrapper up around the filling so that the filling rises slightly above the edge of the wrapper and the side of the dumpling is indented slightly. Place the dumpling on a parchment-paper-lined cookie sheet and top it with a cilantro leaf. Repeat with the remaining ingredients. Cover them with plastic wrap and refrigerate.

To cook the dumplings, bring lots of water to a boil in a saucepan slightly smaller in diameter than your steamer basket. Generously brush the bamboo lattice bottom of the steamer basket with peanut or sesame oil. Fill the basket with the shiu mai—taking care not to overcrowd them. Cover the basket with its lid, reduce the heat to maintain a brisk simmer, and place the basket on top of the pot. Steam the shiu mai for 7 to 10 minutes, or until the filling is firm and white. Protect your hands with oven gloves and remove the basket, taking care to avoid any gusts of steam from the pot. Replenish the pot with more water, if necessary, before steaming more batches.

Serve the shiu mai directly from their basket, accompanied by Spicy Soy Dip.

Makes about 4 dozen hors d'oeuvres

Spicy Soy Dip

This simple dip may be made moments before serving, with ingredients that are available in the Asian food section of most supermarkets. You may also want to offer a separate bowl of plain, light soy sauce for those who don't want the spice.

3/4 cup light soy sauce

1/4 cup rice vinegar, or white vinegar

1 tablespoon hot chili oil

Stir the ingredients together in a bowl. Serve immediately.

Makes about 1 cup

Assorted Asian Pickles

Set out a large tray with a variety of Asian pickles—bought in jars from the Asian food section of your market. Some Asian markets even offer their own freshly made pickles.

Among the best choices are the assorted Korean pickles that generally go by the name *kim chee*. The term actually refers to bok choy pickled with hot chili paste; but you'll also find various other Korean pickles—radish, turnip, bean sprouts, seaweed, and so on—with varying degrees of hotness.

Japanese pickles offer another great range of choices. There are various kinds of Japanese pickled ginger, radish, and plums along with everything from cucumbers to melon slices to miniature eggplants.

Choose a range of colors, shapes and flavors to make an attractive and appetizing tray.

Vietnamese Spring Rolls

Made with thin rice-paper wrappers, which are available in Asian markets, these spring rolls are lighter and crisper than the more familiar Chinese variety. You can also find the cellophane noodles and shiitake mushrooms in Asian markets.

You can fill and wrap the spring rolls a few hours ahead of time, keeping them covered and refrigerated until you fry them.

Arrange the spring rolls on a napkin-lined tray with a bowl of Nuoc Cham Sauce in the center for dipping.

1 ounce cellophane noodles

10 shiitake mushrooms

3/4 pound ground chicken

2 medium scallions, green parts only, cut lengthwise into shreds then crosswise into 1-inch pieces

2 medium garlic cloves, finely chopped

1 small carrot, shredded

2 tablespoons chopped fresh cilantro

1 1/2 tablespoons chopped fresh mint

1/2 tablespoon finely chopped fresh ginger

1/4 teaspoon freshly ground black pepper

2 eggs, well beaten

10 dried rice-paper wrappers

1 1/2 cups vegetable oil

In separate bowls, soak the cellophane noodles and the shiitake mushrooms in enough cold water to cover for about 10 minutes. Drain the noodles well and cut them with scissors into pieces about 1 1/2 inches long. Cut off the stems from the shiitakes and cut the caps crosswise into thin slivers.

In a bowl, combine the noodles and shiitakes with the chicken, scallions, garlic, carrot, cilantro, mint, ginger and pepper, stirring until thoroughly mixed.

With a sharp knife, cut the circular rice papers into 4 equal quarters. On a work surface, brush a quarter-piece of rice paper with beaten egg to soften it. Spread about 2 teaspoons of the filling in a line along the curved side of the paper; fold the 2 ends of the curved side over it, then roll up the egg roll toward the pointed corner of the paper to make a neat, compact cylinder. Continue with the remaining filling and wrappers.

Put the oil in a skillet large enough to hold all the spring rolls. Place the rolls in the oil and put the skillet over medium heat. When the oil heats up, fry the spring rolls, carefully turning them with tongs every few minutes, until crisp and golden, about 30 minutes. Drain on paper towels before transferring to a cloth-napkin-lined serving platter. Serve with Nuoc Cham Sauce.

Makes about 40 spring rolls

Nuoc Cham Sauce

Serve this salty, spicy sauce—based on Vietnamese fish sauce, *nuoc mam*—as an accompaniment to the spring rolls. After handling the chili, be sure to wash your hands thoroughly with soap and water, and take care not to touch your eyes.

Nuoc cham sauce may be made several hours in advance.

3 garlic cloves, peeled

1 fresh hot red chili pepper, split, seeded, membranes removed

2 tablespoons sugar

1/2 lime

6 tablespoons Vietnamese fish sauce (nuoc mam)

1/2 cup water

In a small food processor fitted with the metal blade, or using a mortar and pestle, process or pound together the garlic, chili and sugar into a smooth paste.

Squeeze the lime into the paste. With a small spoon, scoop out the lime pulp and add it, being careful to remove any seeds. Stir in the fish sauce and water to make a smooth sauce. Refrigerate, tightly covered, until serving.

Makes about 1 cup

Lamb Tikka Sticks

These spicy Indian kebabs are served with a cooling yogurt sauce. Start marinating the lamb the night before your party, then skewer it an hour or more in advance and grill the kebabs once guests arrive.

Arrange the skewers of lamb on a metal serving tray, with a bowl of Mint Raita to one side.

3 medium garlic cloves

1/2 medium onion

1 tablespoon coarsely chopped fresh ginger

1/2 tablespoon paprika

1 teaspoon sugar

1 teaspoon ground cumin

1/2 teaspoon ground cardamom

1/2 teaspoon hot chili powder

1/2 cup plain yogurt, regular or low-fat

2 1/2 pounds lean lamb, trimmed and cut into 1-inch cubes

Salt

In a processor fitted with the metal blade, process the garlic, onion and ginger until finely chopped (or pound it with a mortar and pestle); add the paprika, sugar, cumin, cardamom, chili and yogurt and mix well.

In a mixing bowl, combine the lamb with the mixture. Cover with plastic wrap and marinate overnight in the refrigerator.

Soak 30 small bamboo skewers in water for about 1 hour. Thread a couple of cubes of lamb on each skewer. Cover both ends of each skewer with a piece of foil to prevent them from burning.

Preheat the grill or broiler until very hot. Sprinkle the lamb lightly with salt and grill it close to the heat for 2 to 3 minutes per side until nicely charred but still pink inside. Slip the foil off the skewers and serve the kebabs.

Makes 30 skewers

Mint Raita

Prepare the raita several hours in advance and refrigerate, covered.

2 cups plain yogurt, regular or low-fat

1/4 cup loosely packed, finely chopped fresh mint

Salt

In a glass or ceramic bowl, stir together the yogurt and mint. Cover and refrigerate.

Before serving, season the yogurt to taste with a little salt.

Makes about 2 cups

Hot Indonesian Peanut Dip with Fresh Vegetables

This surprising dip is most often used as a salad dressing in Indonesia. It is hot in two different senses—from the chili that seasons it, and because of the temperature at which it is served. Prepare it just before guests arrive.

The shrimp sauce or paste can be found in the Asian food section of a well-stocked supermarket, or in an Asian market.

Serve the dip in a chafing dish over a low flame. Or put it out in a small, heavy heat-proof bowl and replenish the bowl regularly with more hot dip from the kitchen. Surround it with an abundance of fresh seasonal vegetables prepared for dipping.

2 medium garlic cloves

1 fresh hot red or green chili pepper, split, seeded, membranes removed

2 teaspoons chopped fresh ginger

1 teaspoon Indonesian shrimp sauce or paste

2 tablespoons vegetable oil

2 cups crunchy-style peanut butter

1 cup cold water

3 tablespoons canned coconut cream

2 tablespoons lemon juice

Fresh vegetables such as blanched snow peas, jicama sticks, trimmed scallions, carrot sticks, broccoli and cauliflower florets, cucumber spears, blanched green beans, whole raw mushrooms, zucchini sticks and red, green and yellow bell pepper slices

In a food processor fitted with the metal blade, process the garlic, chili, ginger and shrimp sauce into a smooth paste (or pound it with a mortar and pestle).

In a medium saucepan, heat the oil over medium heat. Add the paste and cook, stirring, for about 1 minute. Then reduce the heat slightly and add the peanut butter, 1/2 cup of the water, the coconut cream and the lemon juice. Cook the mixture, stirring continuously, until it is smooth and heated through.

Serve with fresh vegetables for dipping.

Makes about 3 cups

Hot Sake and Assorted Asian Beers

Sake, Japanese rice wine, is often thought of by Westerners as some sort of generic stuff they serve in Japanese restaurants. In fact, there's tremendous variety in sake, and different brands may be described with the same range of adjectives used for grape wines: dry, sweet, light, full-bodied, complex, clean, delicate, and so on. For the purposes of an hors d'oeuvre menu, go for a fairly light, dry sake—Chiyoda, Fu-Ki, Genji, Hakutsuru, Ozeki, Sawanotsuru and Sho-Chiku-Bai are some of the export brands that will fill the bill.

Sake is most often sipped warm, poured from small vaselike pitchers called *tokkuri* into small cups. Very inexpensive *tokkuri* and cups are readily found in Japanese markets, and sometimes even come packaged with sake; but you may substitute any small heat-proof pitcher and demitasse cups. Don't make the mistake of overheating the sake, which makes it taste too sweet and syrupy. Pour it from the bottle into the pitchers, then warm the pitchers in a pan of water kept just below a simmer; the ideal temperature is no more than 140°. Many Japanese also drink sake at room temperature, so don't feel honor-bound to heat it.

And by now we're all familiar with the merits of Asian beer. Keep a range of different brands on hand for your guests, so they'll have a chance to taste and compare. Here are some good brands of beer to seek out: from China, Tsingtao; from Japan, Kirin, Sapporo, Suntory and Asahi; from the Philippines, San Miguel; from Singapore, Tiger; from Thailand, Singha and Amarit; from Korea, OB and Crown. Check your best-stocked local liquor merchant for any new Asian beers that are being imported and add them to the list.

Swedish
Smorgasbord

*T*his modestly named "bread-and-butter table" is anything but modest. In Sweden, any self-respecting smorgasbord will hold a vast array of herrings and other seafoods, a bounty of cold cuts and salads and a trencherman's delight of hearty meat dishes, hot and cold. Smorgasbords are meant to overwhelm the eyes and tempt every tastebud.

But the beauty of serving a smorgasbord as an appetizer buffet is how little cooking you actually have to do. So many of the foods are bought already cooked and are meant to be served cold, and most of the preparation consists of slicing and arranging the foods in whatever artful presentation strikes your fancy.

Set your table with a crisp white cloth and dishware in shades of blue and white, or made of glass, to evoke the cool, clean look of Scandinavian design; add a few wooden accents, such as a carving board, on which to present the open-faced sandwiches, and a few simple, lively flowers—daisies would be perfect. Add the icy, yet romantic, sounds of your favorite Scandinavian composer—Grieg, Sibelius, Nielsen—or the lively pop of ABBA or the cool control of Bach keyboard compositions.

© Felicia Martinez/PhotoEdit

M E N U

Assorted Herrings

Smoked Salmon with Mustard-Honey-Dill Mayonnaise

Cucumber Boats with Bay Shrimp

Open-Faced Mini Sandwiches

Beet and Potato Salad in Baby Lettuce Cups

Swedish Meatballs

Iced Aquavit and Beer

Serves 12

Assorted Herrings

No need to do any kind of cooking here: Delis and supermarkets stock so many different kinds of pickled herrings, loose and packed in jars, that all you have to do is pick out the kind you like.

Among the best-known styles are Bismarck, fresh herrings marinated in vinegar with onions, chilis and juniper berries; Glassblower's, marinated in vinegar with onions, carrots, horseradish and bay leaves; Matjes—"maidens"—herrings, small fillets cured in a salt-and-sugar brine; and Rollmops, fillets rolled around onions and gherkins and then marinated

Smoked Salmon with Mustard-Honey-Dill Mayonnaise

This simple preparation reflects the flavors of the popular Swedish marinated salmon dish, gravlax, without the days of marinating. Make it up to 1 hour in advance.

1/2 cup mayonnaise

3 tablespoons finely chopped fresh dill

2 tablespoons honey, at room temperature

2 tablespoons whole-grain Dijon-style mustard

18 one-ounce long, thin slices smoked salmon

Whole dill sprigs, for garnish

Stir together the mayonnaise, dill, honey and mustard.

A slice at a time, lightly spread one side of the salmon with the mayonnaise mixture. Roll up the slice tightly into a long cylinder and, with a sharp knife, slice the cylinder crosswise into 4 equal pieces. Secure each piece with a toothpick.

Keep the salmon and the extra sauce in the refrigerator, covered, until serving time. Put the sauce in a small bowl for dipping and place it at the center of a napkin- or doily-lined tray; arrange the salmon hors d'oeuvres around the bowl and garnish with dill sprigs.

Makes 6 dozen hors d'oeuvres

in spiced vinegar. You'll also find red-wine-marinated herrings, herrings in sour cream with onions, and all kinds of other variations, depending on whatever is most popular in your region.

Buy at least 1½ quarts of herring total, varying the amount depending on how well your guests like fish. Offer at least 2 or 3—4 would be even better—different kinds. An hour or so before serving, cut the fish up into 3- to 4-inch pieces, and arrange each different kind on a bed of lettuce leaves on a separate platter, or on separate sections of the same large tray. Keep the herrings chilled and covered until serving time.

Cucumber Boats with Bay Shrimp

Prepare this simple, refreshing cold hors d'oeuvre no more than half an hour before guests arrive.

4 (8-to-10-inch-long) cucumbers

3/4 cup mayonnaise

6 tablespoons chopped fresh chives

3 tablespoons lemon juice

2½ cups cooked baby bay shrimp

Peel the cucumbers and cut each one in half lengthwise. With a small spoon, neatly scoop out the seeds to leave a deep groove along each cucumber half. Cut the halves crosswise into 2-inch pieces.

Stir together the mayonnaise, 1/4 cup of the chives and the lemon juice, then stir the shrimp together with the mixture. Place a generous tablespoon of the shrimp on each cucumber piece. Garnish the tops with the remaining chives and arrange the hors d'oeuvres on a serving tray.

Makes about 36 boats

Open-Faced Mini Sandwiches

Bread-and-butter sandwiches are the backbone of the smorgasbord spread. These bite-size versions offer guests a variety of tastes.

If you can, buy loaves of miniature, presliced cocktail breads at your delicatessen. Or buy thinly sliced regular loaves and cut each slice into quarters after you butter it.

Prepare the sandwiches about 1 hour before serving.

96 thin slices miniature cocktail bread (rye, wheat, pumpernickel, white or assorted) or 24 thin slices regular-size bread

1 cup unsalted butter, at room temperature

4 large eggs, hard-boiled and peeled

1/4 cup red salmon roe or black lumpfish caviar

1/2 pound prepared chicken liver pâté

24 baby cornichons (small pickles), or 48 thin round slices regular pickled cucumber

1/2 pound blue cheese

24 shelled walnut halves

6 ounces thinly sliced salami

24 pickled baby onions, halved

Generously butter 1 side of each piece of bread; if you're using large slices, cut each into 4 equal squares after buttering.

Carefully cut each egg crosswise into 1/4-inch slices, using an egg slicer if you have one. Select the 24 best slices and place each on top of a slice of buttered bread. Garnish each egg slice with a dollop of caviar.

Generously spread the pâté on top of 24 more slices of buttered bread. Cut each cornichon lengthwise several times, leaving the slices attached at the stem end, and fan out a cornichon on top of each pâté-topped sandwich; or arrange 2 regular pickle slices on top.

Cut the blue cheese into 24 equal, roughly square pieces and place each on top of another slice of bread. Garnish each square of cheese with a walnut half, gently pressing it down.

Finally, distribute the salami slices on top of the remaining slices of bread. Garnish each with 2 pickled onion pieces, cut sides down.

Arrange the sandwiches in an attractive pattern on a large square or rectangular serving tray or cutting board. Keep at a cool room temperature.

Makes 96 sandwiches

Beet and Potato Salad in Baby Lettuce Cups

Prepare the salad 1 to 2 hours in advance, then spoon it into the lettuce cups shortly before guests arrive.

2 eight-ounce jars diced pickled beets, drained

2 cups boiled potatoes cut into 1/2-inch cubes

1 cup mayonnaise

1 medium onion, finely chopped

1/2 cup chopped fresh parsley

Salt and freshly ground black pepper

24 small leaves butter lettuce

24 small fresh parsley sprigs

In a mixing bowl, stir together the beets, potatoes, mayonnaise, onion and chopped parsley. Season to taste with salt and pepper. Cover and refrigerate.

Before serving, arrange the lettuce leaves like cups on a serving tray or platter. Spoon the salad into the leaves, mounding it in the centers. Garnish with parsley sprigs.

Makes 24 individual lettuce cups

Swedish Meatballs

No smorgasbord would be complete without them. Prepare the meatball mixture up to 2 hours before you fry them. Keep them warm on a hot plate or in a chafing dish for serving.

1 medium onion, finely chopped

1 large boiling potato, grated

2 large eggs, lightly beaten

1/2 pound lean ground beef

1/2 pound ground veal

1/2 pound ground pork

1/4 cup dry bread crumbs

1/4 cup heavy cream

3 tablespoons finely chopped fresh parsley

1 teaspoon salt

1 teaspoon freshly ground black pepper

1/4 cup vegetable oil

In a mixing bowl, combine the onion, potato, eggs, beef, veal, pork, bread crumbs, cream, parsley, salt and pepper, stirring vigorously until they are thoroughly blended and the mixture is light and airy.

With a tablespoon, scoop up the mixture and, with moistened hands, form it into neat balls, placing them on a tray lined with wax paper. Cover with another sheet of wax paper and refrigerate.

Shortly before guests arrive, heat the oil in a large, heavy skillet. Fry the meatballs in several batches without overcrowding, turning them gently several times for 10 to 12 minutes until they are evenly browned and cooked through. Drain on paper towels and keep warm in a low oven until all the meatballs are done.

Serve them from a chafing dish or heated serving platter. Have a jar of toothpicks alongside for guests who don't want to use a fork or fingers.

Makes about 6 dozen meatballs

Iced Aquavit and Beer

Aquavit means "water of life," and after a few bracing sips of this clear, herb-infused liquor, you'll agree that the name fits.

It is meant to be served ice-cold, sipped from small shots. The bottle can be kept in the freezer prior to the party, and may even be frozen in a block of ice (see the instructions for Vodka on page 139).

A word of warning, though. Aquavit can be potent stuff, and it's deceptively easy to drink; so, for your guests' safety, keep an eye on the flow of the liquor, and don't offer *too* much of it. To quench your guests' thirst, particularly after eating the salty herrings, offer a selection of good Scandinavian beers—such as Carlsberg, Ringnes or Tuborg—along with sparkling water or other soft drinks.

Courtesy of Williams-Sonoma

Spanish
Tapas

Centuries ago, it became the custom in Spanish inns to present a glass of sherry with a little lid—tapa—of sliced Serrano ham, Manchego cheese, chorizo or other savory delectable. From this simple practice has grown the early evening feast known as tapas—an array of savory little dishes accompanied by sherry, sangria, wine or beer.

A rustic, old-fashioned air still clings to tapas, and the dishes served have an honest simplicity that translates into easy preparation for the home cook. That's not to say that there's anything simple about the flavors—tapas are generally bold in taste, and it's a good idea to invite only those friends who are certified garlic lovers!

If your dining table or sideboard is made of a richly toned wood—mahogany or rosewood, for example—polish it up and leave it uncovered; or use an old-fashioned lace tablecloth, or plain linen in deep earth colors like burgundy or brown. Present the food on earth-toned or plain white china or earthenware platters, accented with a few ornate silver serving trays if you have them. Set out a stack of small individual plates on which guests can place whatever tapas they select. To further set the mood, some flamenco music or—if you and your friends are so inclined—a Julio Iglesias record would be in order.

M E N U

Traditional Tapas Platter

Shrimp with Green Mayonnaise

Deep-Fried Squid

Steamed Mussels with Saffron Cream

Garlic Chicken

Tortilla Española

Marinated Mushrooms in Sherry Vinaigrette

Baby Artichoke Hearts with Ham

Sherry Tasting and Sangria

Serves 16

Traditional Tapas Platter

Without fail, you'll find a platter of Serrano ham, Manchego cheese and chorizo in any tapas spread, accompanied by slices of crusty bread and green Spanish olives.

Serrano ham is Spain's answer to prosciutto—a raw, air-cured ham served in paper-thin slices. If your local deli doesn't stock it, substitute a good prosciutto. Ask for 1 to 1½ pounds for 16 people, depending on your guests' fondness for ham, and have it sliced as thinly as possible.

Manchego is a hard, sheep's milk cheese, reminiscent of a good Italian Pecorino (which is an acceptable substitute). Order 1 to 1½ pounds, sliced as thinly as possible.

Seek out a good, spicy, dried Spanish or Mexican chorizo or a spicy Italian cured pork sausage (make sure that whatever you buy is cured rather than fresh). Buy 1 to 1½ pounds, and ask for it to be cut at an angle into thin oblong slices.

Up to 2 hours ahead, arrange the Serrano ham, Manchego and chorizo on a large platter, overlapping the slices in a decorative pattern. Serve a bowl of large, unpitted green olives alongside—32 to 40 are sufficient. And accompany the platter with a large basket of crusty peasant bread—a French or sourdough loaf is fine—cut into 1/2-inch-thick slices. Allow at least 3 slices per person.

Shrimp with Green Mayonnaise

Arrange the shrimp on a large circular platter, with the mayonnaise in a bowl at the center for dipping. And let your guests enjoy this wonderful Spanish dish.

64 medium raw shrimp (about 4 pounds)

2 cups dry white wine

3 medium garlic cloves, peeled

1 large whole egg, at room temperature

1 large egg yolk, at room temperature

2 tablespoons lemon juice, at room temperature

3/4 teaspoon dry mustard

1/2 teaspoon salt

1/2 teaspoon freshly ground white pepper

1¹/4 cups olive oil, at room temperature

1/2 cup packed fresh parsley

About 3 hours ahead of time, bring a large pot of water to a boil and cook the shrimp in their shells, in batches if necessary, for about 3 minutes, until they turn bright pink. Drain them well, then rinse them under cold running water until cool enough to handle.

Carefully peel the shrimp, leaving their tails on. With a small, sharp knife, make a shallow incision along their backs, or outer curves, and devein them. Put the shrimp in a bowl, toss them with the wine, cover them with plastic wrap and refrigerate them for 2 hours, turning them occasionally in the wine.

About 1 hour before the party, put the garlic in a food processor with the metal blade. Process it until it is finely chopped, stopping several times to scrape down the bowl. Add the whole egg, egg yolk, lemon juices, mustard, salt and pepper and process the mixture until smooth.

With the machine running, slowly pour in the oil in a thin, steady stream; as the mayonnaise begins to thicken and increase in volume, increase the flow of oil, continuing until it has been fully incorporated.

Add the parsley and process it until it has been fully blended into the mayonnaise. Chill in a covered bowl until serving.

Makes 16 servings

Deep-Fried Squid

Ask your fishmonger to clean the squid for you when you buy it.

Have the flour seasoned and the squid cut up and ready in advance. Heat the oil when guests start arriving, and cook the squid in several batches so some is always hot and crisp.

1¹/2 cups dry white wine

2 pounds medium fresh squid, thoroughly cleaned

3/4 cup all-purpose flour

1/2 teaspoon salt

1/2 teaspoon freshly ground black pepper

1/2 teaspoon cayenne pepper

Vegetable oil for deep frying

8 large lemons, cut into quarter wedges

Cut the squid bodies into 1/2-inch-wide rings and the tentacles into 2-inch pieces.

Put the flour, salt, black pepper and cayenne in a paper bag; close the bag tightly and shake well.

In a deep, heavy skillet or deep fryer, heat at least 3 inches of oil to a temperature of 375° (use a deep-frying thermometer).

Spread the flour mixture on a large plate. Dredge a batch of squid pieces in the flour until lightly but evenly coated. Carefully add them to the oil and fry until golden brown, about 2 minutes; remove with a wire skimmer and drain on paper towels. Fry the squid in batches that won't overcrowd the deep fryer.

Serve the squid on a napkin-lined platter, accompanied by lemon wedges for guests to squeeze over their servings.

Makes 16 servings

Steamed Mussels with Saffron Cream

Mussels are a popular tapas feature and are partnered here with the definitive Spanish spice—saffron.

Buy only absolutely fresh mussels with tightly closed shells, from a reputable fish market; if the mussels smell at all fishy, avoid them. Once they're cooked, discard any that haven't opened.

Since the mussels are served cold, they may be prepared 1 to 2 hours before guests arrive.

1 1/2 cups dry white wine

2 medium garlic cloves, finely chopped

1/2 medium onion, finely chopped

1 sprig fresh or 1 teaspoon dried tarragon

1 bay leaf

64 large black mussels, cleaned, bearded and scrubbed

2 cups heavy cream

1 teaspoon saffron threads

Salt and freshly ground white pepper

2 canned pimientos, drained and cut into 1/4-inch squares

Put the wine, garlic, onion, tarragon and bay leaf in a large, wide pot and bring it all to a boil over high heat. Reduce the heat to medium, add the mussels, cover tightly and steam until their shells open, about 5 minutes. Remove the mussels from the pot and set them aside.

Line a strainer with cheesecloth and set it over a medium saucepan. Pour the mussel cooking liquid through the cheesecloth. Bring the liquid to a boil over high heat and continue boiling 7 to 10 minutes until it reduces to about 1/2 cup. Add the cream and saffron and continue boiling 10 to 12 minutes more until the mixture thickens and reduces to about 1 1/3 cups. Remove the pan from the heat and season to taste with salt and white pepper.

When the mussels are cool enough to handle, remove the empty shell halves, leaving shells containing the mussel meat; discard any unopened or odd-looking mussels. Arrange the mussels in their shells in a neat pattern on a large serving platter. Nap each mussel in its shell with the saffron cream sauce. Let the mussels cool to room temperature, then cover them with plastic wrap and put them in the refrigerator.

Before serving, dot each mussel with a piece of pimiento.

Garlic Chicken

Prepare the ingredients an hour or two ahead of time and have them ready to cook when guests arrive. Serve it directly from the skillet, or transfer it to a heated serving dish; be sure to place it on top of plenty of hot pads to protect the table. Accompany the chicken with lots of bread that guests can use to sop up the sauce.

2 pounds skinless, boneless chicken breasts, cut into 1-inch chunks

1/4 teaspoon salt

1/4 teaspoon freshly ground black pepper

1/4 cup all-purpose flour

1/2 cup olive oil

1/4 cup unsalted butter

4 medium garlic cloves, coarsely chopped

Season the chicken pieces with salt and pepper and sprinkle them lightly and evenly with the flour.

In a large skillet, heat the olive oil with the butter over medium heat. As soon as the butter foams, add the chicken pieces and the garlic. Sauté, stirring frequently, for 7 to 10 minutes, until the chicken pieces are cooked through and light golden brown.

Present this dish with a spoon so guests can serve themselves some of the garlicky sauce.

Tortilla Española

This filling, traditional flat potato-and-onion omelet is served lukewarm or cold, cut into wedges. Its mild flavor is a nice contrast to the spicier dishes of the tapas buffet.

Prepare the tortilla 1½ hours or more before the party.

2 pounds boiling potatoes, peeled and cut crosswise into several pieces

1/2 cup olive oil

3/4 pound sweet onion, cut crosswise into thin slices

2 medium garlic cloves, finely chopped

10 eggs

1 teaspoon salt

1/2 teaspoon freshly ground white pepper

1/4 cup chopped fresh parsley

Put the potatoes in a large saucepan with enough cold water to cover. Bring them to a boil and cook 15 to 20 minutes, just until the potatoes can be easily pierced with the tip of a small, sharp knife. Drain them well and rinse them under cold running water until they are cool enough to handle.

While the potatoes are boiling, heat 2 tablespoons of the olive oil in a skillet over medium heat. Add the onions and garlic and sauté 5 to 7 minutes until translucent and tender.

In a large mixing bowl, beat the eggs with the salt and pepper until frothy. Cut the potatoes crosswise into thin slices and add them in the bowl with the onion mixture and the parsley, stirring gently to combine them without breaking up the potatoes too much.

Distribute all but 2 tablespoons of the remaining oil evenly between 2 heavy, deep 8-inch ovenproof skillets with sloping sides (if you have only 1 such skillet, prepare the tortilla half at a time from this point on). Heat the skillets over medium high-heat, then put half of the tortilla mixture in each and immediately turn the heat down as low as possible. Smooth the surface of the mixture and cover the skillets with their lids or large heat proof plates.

Cook the tortillas until the egg has set in the center, about 15 minutes. Carefully unmold each tortilla onto the lid or plate. Add the remaining oil to the skillets and raise the heat slightly; then slip the tortillas back into the skillets, reduce the heat, and cook them on their other sides for 3 to 4 minutes more.

Remove them from the heat and let the tortillas cool in their skillets to room temperature. Unmold them and cut each tortilla into 8 equal wedges. Store the wedges in the refrigerator, covered, until 30 minutes or so before serving time. Arrange them on a serving platter.

Makes 16 tortilla wedges

Marinated Mushrooms in Sherry Vinaigrette

Marinated in good Spanish sherry vinegar and olive oil, these mushrooms are wonderfully tangy and succulent. Make them up to 2 days ahead.

2 cups sherry vinegar

3/4 cup olive oil

3 bay leaves

2 garlic cloves, unpeeled but smashed

1/4 cup granulated sugar

1 teaspoon whole allspice berries

1 teaspoon whole white peppercorns

1/4 teaspoon salt

2 pounds small-to-medium mushrooms

In a large, nonreactive saucepan, bring the vinegar, olive oil, bay leaves, garlic, sugar, allspice, salt and pepper to a boil. Add the mushrooms, reduce the heat and simmer gently for about 10 minutes.

Empty the mushrooms and their liquid into a heat proof bowl or glass jar. Let cool to room temperature, then cover and refrigerate up to 2 days (but at least overnight) before serving. Drain the mushrooms and heap them in a serving bowl. Serve chilled.

Makes 4 cups

Baby Artichoke Hearts with Ham

In spring and summer look for tiny, baby artichokes in the supermarket. Stem, pare and cut up the artichokes an hour or two before the party, keeping them in a bowl of cold water into which you've squeezed fresh lemon to keep them from discoloring. Then drain them well, pat them dry and cook them up in batches if necessary, as guests arrive.

Serve the artichokes right from the skillet, accompanied by plenty of bread for guests to dip in the oil.

2 lemons

4 pounds baby artichokes

2 cups olive oil

10 medium garlic cloves, coarsely chopped

1/2 pound Serrano ham or prosciutto, thinly sliced and cut into 1/4-inch-wide strips

Freshly ground black pepper

An hour or so before guests arrive, squeeze the lemons into a large bowl of cold water. One at a time, strip the leaves from the artichokes and pare off their tough green skins, leaving the tender, pale green artichoke hearts. Cut the hearts into quarters or halves, depending on size, and put them in the bowl of water until you're ready to cook them.

Drain the hearts well and pat them dry with kitchen towels or paper towels.

Heat the oil in a large skillet over medium heat. Add the hearts and garlic and sauté 5 to 7 minutes, stirring frequently, until they are tender and lightly browned. Scatter in the ham about 2 minutes before the artichokes are done. Season with black pepper to taste.

Sherry Tasting

Sherry is the traditional drink to serve with tapas. Offer guests a variety of imported Spanish sherries—ranging from bone-dry *finos* through richer and sweeter *amontillados* and *olorosos* to the sweet, honeylike cream sherries. Choose from the many fine labels available—including Domecq, Harvey's, Osborne, De Terry, Gonzalez Byass, Williams & Humbert, Sandeman, and Bobadilla.

Serve the sherry at cool room temperature. (But do have ice on hand for any guests who might like theirs on the rocks.) If you have traditional small sherry glasses, which hold no more than about 3 ounces, use them for service (substituting large wine glasses for guests who want theirs iced). Don't pour too much at one time; sherry is meant for sipping.

Sangria

You might call this the original wine cooler. Deceptively mild, it's a quite potent concoction.

Mix the sangria an hour or two ahead of time, and add the soda just when guests arrive. Have ice cubes or, preferably, a large block of ice, on hand to chill the sangria at serving time.

4 bottles dry red wine

2 cups oloroso or amontillado sherry

1¹/₂ cups triple sec

1 cup brandy

3/4 cup sugar

5 large oranges

5 large lemons

4 large peaches or 6 nectarines, peeled and sliced

6 cups club soda

In a large punch bowl, stir together the wine, sherry, triple sec, brandy and sugar. Cut 1 orange and 1 lemon in half and squeeze them in; thinly slice the remaining oranges and lemons and add them with the peaches or nectarines to the bowl.

Just when guests arrive, stir in the club soda and add the ice.

Makes about 1¹/₂ gallons

Wild
Cajun Tastes

*V*ividly colorful, rich and spicy, Cajun food is among America's most seductive and exciting cuisines, combining the most lively elements of French, Spanish, English, African and Native American culinary traditions.

The morsels that make up this buffet are marvelously conducive to lively partying. Serve them at Mardi Gras time, during the fall football season, for a special occasion or for no reason other than to gather good friends together.

You'll need to do a fair amount of advance preparation for the menu—turning artichokes, mixing batters, stuffing oysters. But, that done, you're free to have a good ol' time, except for a few stints of frying during the party.

As diverse as the cultural influences on New Orleans are, you're free to set your table in any number of ways: use your most elegant china, crystal and silver; rustic earthenware and time-blackened cast iron; or all the glitz, glitter and color of a Mardi Gras festival. Just be sure to lay on a good supply of New Orleans sounds—especially the lively beat of the music known as Zydeco.

M E N U

Shrimp Remoulade in Artichoke Bottoms

Oysters Bienville

Steamed Crayfish with Cayenne Butter

Deep-Fried Okra

Stuffed Eggs Creole

Andouille

Mushrooms with Tasso and Bread Crumb Stuffing

Ice Cold Beer

Serves 16

Shrimp Remoulade in Artichoke Bottoms

A classic French remoulade with a hint of Cajun spice enhances tiny bay shrimp in this appetizer salad.

Prepare the artichoke bottoms several hours in advance, and keep them in a large bowl of water into which you've squeezed a whole lemon, which will keep them from discoloring. You can also mix up the Shrimp Remoulade ahead of time. Shortly before guests arrive, drain the artichoke bottoms, pat them dry and fill them with the shrimp mixture.

2 dozen medium artichokes (3 to 4 inches wide at the base), washed, stems snapped off at the base

1 lemon, halved

1 cup mayonnaise

1/2 cup finely chopped fresh scallions

1/2 cup finely chopped celery

1/2 cup chopped fresh parsley

3 tablespoons creamy Dijon-style mustard

1 tablespoon chopped fresh tarragon leaves, or 1 teaspoon dried tarragon

2 teaspoons sugar

1/2 tablespoon cayenne

3 cups cooked baby bay shrimp

2 lemons, thinly sliced, slices cut in half

Bring a very large pot of water to a boil. Add the artichokes and boil them for about 15 minutes, until the tip of a small knife easily pierces their bases.

Drain the artichokes well and rinse them under cold running water. When they are cool enough to handle, prepare them one at a time. First, fill a large bowl with cold water and squeeze both lemon halves into it. Starting at the base of an artichoke, remove its leaves, pulling each leaf downward, until only a cone of leaves rising from the widest point of the artichoke remains. Then cut off that top cone of leaves to reveal the fibrous choke inside the bottom. With a sharp-edged spoon, scrape out the choke to form a natural cup. Finally, with a small, sharp knife, pare the tough skin from around the outside of the artichoke bottom, and trim the base flat; put the artichoke bottom in the bowl of water. Repeat this step with the remaining artichokes.

To make the remoulade, stir together the mayonnaise, scallions, celery, parsley, mustard, tarragon, sugar and cayenne. Stir the shrimp into this sauce, cover and refrigerate.

Shortly before guests arrive, drain the artichokes and pat them dry with paper towels. Spoon the shrimp remoulade mixture into the bottoms and place them on a serving tray. Garnish each with a half-slice of lemon, twisted.

Makes 32 hors d'oeuvres

Oysters Bienville

This rich baked oyster dish is named after the French colonial governor who founded New Orleans in 1718.

You can make the Bienville sauce an hour or two in advance. Most good suppliers can prepare the oysters for you on the half shell, and pack them on crushed ice for you to carry home; you may, however, have to bring your own containers. To open oysters yourself, use a special oyster knife with a sharp, short, sturdy blade. Holding the oyster in a folded kitchen towel to protect your hand from the knife, with the flat side of the shell up, carefully insert the blade between the shell halves and lever the shell open. Cut the oyster free from the top half and discard this part of the shell. Slide the blade under the bottom of the oyster to free it from the shell, but leave the oyster sitting there in its nectar.

A note of caution. With so much of our coastal waters now polluted, be sure to buy your oysters only from the most reputable purveyors. If the oysters look or smell at all suspicious, do *not* buy them.

1/4 cup unsalted butter

6 large mushrooms, finely chopped

2 medium garlic cloves, finely chopped

1/4 cup all-purpose flour

3 cups half-and-half

1 cup cooked bay shrimp, finely chopped

1/2 cup finely chopped parsley

1/4 cup dry sherry

2 teaspoons cayenne

1 teaspoon salt

2 egg yolks, lightly beaten

48 oysters on the half shell

In a medium saucepan, melt the butter over medium heat. Add the mushrooms and garlic and sauté 3 to 5 minutes, then sprinkle in the flour and continue sautéing, stirring continuously with a wire whisk, for 3 to 5 minutes more.

Whisk the half-and-half into the saucepan. Bring to a boil, stirring constantly until the sauce thickens; then reduce the heat to low and simmer gently for 5 to 7 minutes more.

Remove the sauce from the heat and stir in the shrimp, parsley, sherry, cayenne, salt and egg yolks until smooth.

Preheat the oven to 400°. Fill several shallow baking dishes with rock salt, and nestle the oysters into the salt.

Spoon the sauce generously over the oysters in the shells, covering them completely. Bake for about 15 minutes, until the sauce is hot and bubbly. Serve directly from the baking dish, setting it on a hot pad on the serving table.

Makes 48 hors d'oeuvres

Steamed Crayfish with Cayenne Butter

Steam these up fresh in several batches, and save your guests most of the messy work by twisting off the tails and cracking them in the kitchen. Nevertheless, have individual finger bowls at hand so guests can dip their digits after they've indulged in this Cajun specialty.

You may have to order the live crayfish specially from your local fishmonger; check with him well in advance of the party.

1 bottle dry white wine

3 cups water

2 bay leaves

1 teaspoon white peppercorns

12 pounds live crayfish

1 cup unsalted butter

2 teaspoons cayenne

In a large pot, bring the wine and water to a boil with the bay leaves and peppercorns. Add about 1/4 of the crayfish and cook them, covered, for 4 to 5 minutes.

With a large wire skimmer, remove the crayfish from the pot; do not discard the liquid in the pot. Protecting your hands with kitchen towels, twist off and discard the crayfish heads. Squeeze each crayfish tail between your fingers to crack it.

In a small saucepan, melt the butter and stir in the cayenne. Pour the melted, seasoned butter into a small bowl.

Set the bowl of butter in the middle of a serving tray and arrange the cracked crayfish tails around it. Place the tray on the buffet table, and let your guests peel the crayfish tails and dip them in the butter. As the supply of crayfish tails decreases, cook and prepare more and replenish the tray.

Makes 10 pounds

Deep-Fried Okra

Okra is the classic Southern vegetable, served here crisply fried in a cornmeal coating.

You can easily coat the okra several hours in advance and store it in the refrigerator. Cook the okra in several batches.

1 1/2 cups fine cornmeal

1 cup all-purpose flour

2 teaspoons cayenne pepper

1 teaspoon salt

3 pounds whole fresh okra, trimmed

4 eggs, lightly beaten

Vegetable oil for deep frying

Put the cornmeal, flour, cayenne and salt in a paper or plastic bag, close it tight, and shake it to mix the ingredients thoroughly. Pour out the mixture onto a large plate.

One at a time, dip the okra in the egg to coat it, then roll it in the seasoned cornmeal to cover it evenly. Place the coated okra on a baking sheet lined with wax paper. Repeat this step with the remaining okra. Cover it all with another sheet of wax paper and refrigerate until serving time.

In a large, heavy skillet or deep fryer, heat several inches of oil to 375° (use a deep frying thermometer). Fry as many okra at one time as will fit in the oil without overcrowding, cooking them and turning them with a wire skimmer or slotted spoon 3 to 4 minutes, until golden brown. Drain the okra on paper towel.

Makes 8 dozen bite-size pieces

Stuffed Eggs Creole

A Cajun twist on an hors d'oeuvre standby. Prepare these several hours in advance, keeping them covered and refrigerated until serving time.

16 hard-boiled eggs, halved lengthwise

1/2 cup mayonnaise

1 tablespoon lemon juice

1/2 teaspoon cayenne

5 drops Tabasco™ sauce

1/4 teaspoon salt

2 tablespoons finely chopped fresh chives

2 tablespoons finely chopped fresh parsley

2 tablespoons finely chopped red bell pepper

Slivered pimientos, for garnish

Put the egg yolks in a food processor with the metal blade and add the mayonnaise, lemon juice, cayenne, Tabasco™ and salt. Process this until it is smoothly blended. Add the chives, parsley and bell pepper and pulse just until they're mixed.

Spoon the mixture into a piping bag fitted with a star tip, and pipe it back into the egg white halves. Garnish the yolk mixture with pimiento slivers and arrange them on a serving tray.

Makes 32 stuffed egg halves

Andouille

The spicy smoked pork sausage of New Orleans makes a vividly simple counterpoint to the other dishes. For 16 people, cut 1½ pounds of andouille crosswise into 1/2-inch-thick rounds. Heat a few tablespoons of vegetable oil over medium heat in a heavy skillet and fry them off for 2 to 3 minutes per side. Drain them

briefly on paper towels and transfer them to a serving tray, garnished with bunches of parsley or watercress. Cook and serve them as guests arrive.

Mushrooms with Tasso and Bread Crumb Stuffing

Tasso is the distinctive ham of Cajun cuisine, with a rich, spicy, smoky flavor; if you can't locate it, buy the most highly seasoned smoked ham you can find.

Stuff the mushrooms several hours ahead of time, so they're ready to pop into the oven in batches.

4 dozen large mushrooms, wiped clean with a damp towel

1/2 pound tasso ham, finely chopped

1½ cups coarse soft bread crumbs

1/4 cup chopped fresh parsley

1/4 cup grated Parmesan cheese

1/2 teaspoon dry mustard powder

1 cup unsalted butter, melted

Remove the mushroom stems and chop them finely. In a mixing bowl, stir together the chopped mushroom stems, ham, bread crumbs, parsley, Parmesan and mustard powder. Add the butter and stir until thoroughly blended.

Pack the stuffing into the mushroom

caps, mounding it slightly. Place the mushrooms on a baking sheet lined with wax paper, cover them with another sheet of wax paper and refrigerate until serving time.

Ice Cold Beer

Nothing slakes the thirst brought on by a Cajun feast like great lashings of beer—particularly the New Orleans brands of choice, Dixie or Jax.

Flavors
of the New
Southwest

We've gone past the point at which Southwestern cooking can be called merely the latest rage. This cuisine has evolved far beyond the old Tex-Mex and Cal-Mex specials of tacos, enchiladas, burritos, rice and beans. The startling, satisfying tastes of the new Southwest are here to stay.

This Southwestern hors d'oeuvre buffet is great at any time of year, but I think it's especially fun when the days are longer and it's still sunny at cocktail hour. Set your table near the window and, if you can, use Southwestern-style pottery to serve it. That doesn't necessarily mean rustic, though; in crafts shops and department stores alike, you're likely to find the work of hip young designers inspired by Southwestern colors and motifs. Add the gleam of a silver platter, or of New Mexican Nambe wear. Decorate the table with a few Southwestern artifacts such as kachinas, folk art animals, native pots or painted gourds; or go natural with a few cacti (beware of spines that might hurt guests!) or chunks of sandstone. The perfect music, to my mind, is a recording by the East L.A. Mexican folk-rock group Los Lobos.

127

M E N U

Crab and Green Chile Quesadillas

Scallop Ceviche

Blue Corn Nachos with Chorizo

Spicy Chicken Mini Tacos

Queso Fundido

Guacamole with Fresh Vegetables

Mexican Beer Tasting

Serves 16

© Burke/Triolo

Crab and Green Chile Quesadillas

This is a sophisticated variation on the classic Mexican answer to grilled cheese.

Assemble the quesadillas an hour or two in advance, so they're ready to fry up as guests start arriving. Cook a few at a time, keeping them warm on a heated serving platter.

Let guests top them with sour cream or guacamole if they like.

24 (8-to-10-inch) flour tortillas

1 1/2 pounds Monterey Jack cheese, shredded

In a large skillet or on a large griddle over medium heat, melt 1 tablespoon of the butter for each quesadilla you're about to fry. Carefully transfer 1 or more quesadillas to the skillet or griddle, taking care not to overcrowd them. Fry the tortillas for 1 to 2 minutes, until the underside is browned and crisp, pressing down occasionally with the back of a spatula to make the top tortilla adhere to the bottom as the cheese melts. Then carefully flip each quesadilla and tuck in any filling that falls out; keep frying until the other side is browned.

As each quesadilla is done, transfer it to a cutting board and, with a large, sharp knife, cut it into 6 equal wedges. Transfer the wedges to a heated serving platter and serve them with the sour cream in a bowl alongside for guests who want to add a dollop.

Makes 6 dozen quesadilla wedges

Scallop Ceviche

The lime juice in this recipe essentially "cooks" the scallops through marination.

Buy the largest, freshest sea scallops you can find. Throw the ceviche together so the scallops can marinate 3 to 4 hours before the party begins. Serve the ceviche in a shallow bowl set inside a larger bowl of crushed ice. Place a small glass of cocktail toothpicks alongside so guests can spear the scallops.

Wash your hands thoroughly after handling the hot chiles, and be very careful not to touch your eyes or any cuts; the volatile oils can cause a painful burning sensation.

48 large sea scallops (approximately 3 pounds), trimmed of tough connective tissue

2 medium red onions, coarsely chopped

3 hot green or red chiles, stemmed, seeded and finely chopped

1 cup fresh lime juice

1 1/2 teaspoons salt

1 teaspoon freshly ground white pepper

1/2 cup chopped fresh cilantro

1 head red leaf or other attractive lettuce, leaves separated

In a large glass or ceramic bowl, stir together the scallops, onion, chiles, lime juice, salt and pepper. Cover and refrigerate for 3 to 4 hours, stirring occasionally, until the scallops turn opaque and firm.

Drain off the excess liquid, leaving just a little to keep the scallops moist, and toss the scallops with the cilantro. Line a shallow serving bowl with lettuce leaves and fill with the scallops.

Makes 4 cups

1 1/2 pounds flaked crabmeat

12 canned whole green chiles, torn into 1/4-inch-wide strips

1 1/2 sticks unsalted butter

1 1/2 cups sour cream

Place 12 of the tortillas on a work surface. Using half of the cheese, sprinkle cheese over each one up to 1/2 inch from its rim. Scatter the crabmeat on top of the cheese and evenly distribute the chile strips. Then top the tortillas with the remaining cheese and the remaining tortillas.

Blue Corn Nachos with Chorizo

Blue corn tortilla chips, made from a natural blue corn, are now available in well-stocked supermarkets, though you can also use regular golden tortilla chips. Many markets, as well as Latin American stores, carry spicy chorizo sausage; if you can't find it, substitute hot Italian sausage. And by all means make some nachos with just plain cheese; some of your guests might not want the sausage.

Assemble all the nachos 30 minutes in advance, ready to pop under the broiler in batches as the party progresses.

1¹/₂ pounds chorizo

2 bags blue corn tortilla chips

1¹/₂ pounds Monterey Jack cheese, shredded

Preheat the broiler.

Slit the skin of the chorizo and peel it off. Put the chorizo meat in a large skillet over medium heat and sauté 5 to 7 minutes, until done, stirring the meat and breaking it up with a wooden spoon. Drain off all excess fat.

Select 64 whole, fairly flat tortilla chips, reserving the rest to serve separately. On the concave side of each chip, place a heaping teaspoon of cooked chorizo. Top this with a generous teaspoon of cheese.

As you top each chip, place it on a broiler tray. When the tray is full, broil the nachos 4 to 5 inches from the heat just until the cheese melts and begins to bubble, taking care not to let the edges of the chips burn.

Carefully transfer the nachos to a heated serving platter. Let your guests top the nachos with sour cream or guacamole if they like.

Makes 64 individual nacho chips

Spicy Chicken Mini Tacos

These bite-size tacos are served with a spicy ground chicken mixture. You can assemble them several hours ahead, so they're ready to fry in batches as guests arrive.

Serve them on heated platters, and let your guests garnish them with guacamole if they like.

1/4 cup olive oil

2 large red onions, finely chopped

2 jalapeño chilis, stemmed, seeded and finely chopped

2 medium garlic cloves, finely chopped

3 teaspoons ground cumin

2 teaspoons ground chili powder

1¹/₂ pounds ground chicken

1 teaspoon salt

1/4 cup chopped fresh cilantro leaves

24 (6-to-8-inch) corn tortillas

Vegetable oil for deep frying

Heat the olive oil over medium heat in a large skillet. Add the onion, chilis and garlic and sauté them 3 to 5 minutes, until tender. Add the cumin and chili powder and sauté 30 seconds more. Then add the chicken and salt and sauté about 5 minutes, until cooked through, stirring continuously with a wooden spoon and breaking up the chicken. Pour off any excess fat from the skillet. Stir the cilantro into the chicken mixture.

Stack a few tortillas together and, with a 3-inch cookie cutter, cut 2 mini tortillas from each big one. Place a generous tablespoon of the ground chicken mixture in each mini tortilla, fold it in half over the chicken and secure its edges with 2 wooden toothpicks.

In a large, heavy skillet, heat at least 1 inch of oil to 375° (measure the temperature with a deep-frying thermometer). Without overcrowding the tacos fry them in several batches for 1¹/₂ to 2 minutes, turning them once, until they are golden and crisp. With a wire skimmer or slotted spoon, remove them and drain them well on paper towels. Carefully slip out the toothpicks and serve the tacos on a heated platter.

Makes 48 mini tacos

Queso Fundido

This Mexican version of cheese fondue is served as a dip for tortilla chips or fresh vegetables. Prepare this no more than 30 minutes ahead of time.

3 tablespoons unsalted butter

2 hot green or red chilis, stemmed, seeded and finely chopped

1 medium onion, finely chopped

1 medium garlic clove, finely chopped

2 cups Mexican beer

1 pound Monterey Jack cheese, shredded

1/2 pound sharp cheddar cheese, shredded

1 1/2 tablespoons cornstarch

Salt and freshly ground white pepper

Melt the butter in a chafing dish or fondue pot over medium heat on the stovetop. Add the chilis, onion and garlic and sauté 3 to 5 minutes, until tender. Add the beer and bring it to a boil.

Meanwhile, toss the shredded cheeses with the cornstarch. Reduce the heat to low and gradually stir in the cheese about 1/4 cup at a time, adding more only after the previous addition has melted. Season to taste with salt and white pepper.

Place the dish in a chafing dish over low heat on the serving table, with chips and vegetables nearby. Have a large spoon or ladle at hand for guests to dish up some of the Queso Fundido onto individual plates if they like.

Makes about 6 cups

Guacamole with Fresh Vegetables

Mix the guacamole as close as possible to the time your guests are due; if left too long, the avocado will discolor.

Serve with an assortment of crisp vegetables for dipping—jicama, carrot or celery sticks; zucchini slices; broccoli florets; or other vegetables. Have a large bowl of blue and yellow corn chips on hand, and encourage guests to spoon some guacamole inside their chicken tacos or on their quesadilla wedges.

6 large ripe avocados, preferably the pebbly-skinned Haas variety, halved, seeded and peeled

2 medium, firm, ripe tomatoes, halved, seeded and coarsely chopped

1 medium sweet Vidalia, Walla Walla or Maui onion, or red onion, finely chopped

1/2 cup canned green chilis

6 tablespoons chopped fresh cilantro

1/4 cup sour cream

3 tablespoons fresh lime or lemon juice

Salt and freshly ground white pepper

In a large mixing bowl, mash the avocados coarsely with a fork or a potato masher. Add the tomatoes, onion, chilis, cilantro, sour cream and lime or lemon juice and blend just until well combined, leaving the avocado slightly chunky. Season to taste with salt and pepper.

Makes about 6 cups

Mexican Beer Tasting

This hors d'oeuvre party is a wonderful occasion to offer a comparative sampling of the many fine Mexican beers now widely available.

Offer at least one of the lighter beers—particularly the ever-popular Corona, as well as Hussong's and Carta Blanca. And include some of the gutsier varieties as well—Dos Equis, Leon Negro, Superior or Noche Buena. Serve a dish of lime wedges to guests who want to observe the custom of squeezing one into their beer glass.

Have a supply of chilled, crisp, light white wine—a California Fumé Blanc, for example—and iced mineral water for guests who want to forgo the alcohol.

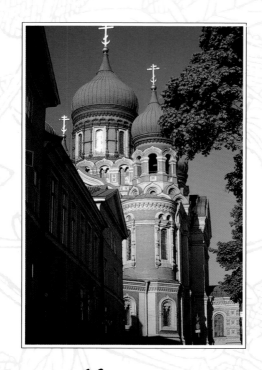

Russian
Caviar Party

A truly special occasion—a promotion, an engagement, an anniversary, a welcome for dear friends or the new year—deserves to be marked with elegance. And there's nothing more elegant than a party featuring ikra, the delicacy of Imperial Russia more commonly known in the West as caviar.

Such an occasion calls for more intimacy than most hors d'oeuvre entertaining—six guests plus the hosts is ideal. But the preparation and execution are so easy that you can certainly invite double or triple that number, or more—provided the budget allows for proportionately more of the precious caviar.

Set out the caviars you've chosen and their accompaniments on the finest table service you have, whether it's crystal, silver, cut glass or fine porcelain; but keep simplicity in mind too, so that nothing detracts from the shimmering beauty of the assorted caviars. Polish the wood of your dining table or sideboard to the deepest sheen; or use a plain white or neutral linen cloth. Have small plates at hand on which guests can prepare their individual bites of blini or bread with caviar. Small hors d'oeuvre forks should be set out as well, though it's perfectly respectable for guests to pop blini into their mouths by hand.

135

M E N U

A Selection of Caviars

Buckwheat Buttermilk Blini

Toast Points and Black Bread

Butter

Sour Cream

Chopped Egg

Snipped Chives

Chopped Sweet Onion

Lemon Wedges

Vodka and Champagne

Serves 8

A Selection of Caviars

Many kinds of excellent salted fish roe are now available in gourmet markets. But the only roe that can truly be called caviar is that of the sturgeon. Good caviar has a clean, delicate, not-too-salty flavor just slightly reminiscent of the sea; if it tastes or smells too fishy, it's past its peak.

Most of the world's classic caviar comes from either the Soviet Union or Iran. *Beluga* caviar, thought by some gourmets to be the finest of all, comes from the beluga sturgeon; it has the largest eggs, which range in color from black to dark pearl gray. *Osetra* or *osetrova* caviar is smaller and darker than beluga; it also has an excellent flavor. *Sevruga* is small, dark roe; some prefer it to beluga. *Malassol* caviar refers to any of the previously mentioned grades sold in the freshest, lightly salted form.

Imported caviars are sold at a premium price that some may find prohibitively expensive. But alternatives do exist that allow for elegant entertaining within a reasonable budget.

Black *American sturgeon* caviar is ever more widely available; it has a refinement of color and flavor that compares favorably to imported varieties. *Pressed caviar* is made from broken or immature sevruga or osetra eggs, and while it is somewhat saltier and certainly less perfect looking, it has some of their premium flavor.

American golden caviar, from whitefish, is a fine, pale golden roe with good, subtle flavor and a wonderful texture. *Salmon caviar*, composed of large, salmon-red eggs, has a distinctive flavor reminiscent of the fish from which it comes. And even humble *lumpfish roe*, colored black with natural food dyes, roughly approximates the caviar experience, though it should be pressed into service only as a last resort.

Allow for at least a good 1/4 cup total of caviar per person; since a teaspoon or so of the roe will go on each blini or piece of toast or bread, that yields a dozen or so individual hors d'oeuvres per guest. If you plan the gathering to last longer than an hour or so, increase the quantities. By all means offer a selection of different roes: perhaps a comparative tasting of the three premium imported varieties for a very upscale occasion; or a beautiful array of different colors and sizes of roe.

Classic caviar servers set the roe in a small bowl held within a larger bowl that's filled with crushed ice. For a caviar assortment, you could, if you like, put crushed ice inside a large platter with sides or a shallow serving bowl, then set matching bowls of roe inside the ice; just make sure the bowls are thick enough so that the cold from the ice doesn't freeze a layer of roe on the inside of the bowls. Alternatively, just set out the roes in matching, well-chilled dishes. In each

dish of caviar, set a small silver, shell or mother-of-pearl serving spoon.

Offer guests a selection of bases on which to spread the caviar—the classic savory pancakes known as blini, along with small, thin triangles of white toast and a good black bread or pumpernickel. Some connoisseurs say that nothing else is needed to highlight the caviar's flavor. But a rich drizzle of melted butter or dollop of sour cream, a squeeze of lemon, or a sprinkling of chives, onion or egg all add delightful variety to the experience. Leave your guests to experiment with their own taste.

Buckwheat Buttermilk Blini

The rich tang of buttermilk complements the sour, earthy taste of buckwheat flour, providing perfect contrast to the flavor of caviar.

Mix up the batter an hour or so before the party and leave it covered at room temperature. Or prepare it the night before and refrigerate it (if you refrigerate the batter, let it sit at room temperature for at least 30 minutes before you cook the blini).

Prepare the blini in several batches, placing them on a heated serving tray or in a napkin-lined basket to keep them warm. Replenish them with freshly made blini as the party continues.

3/4 cup buckwheat flour

1/2 cup all-purpose flour

1 teaspoon baking powder

1/2 teaspoon salt

1 1/2 cups buttermilk

2 tablespoons unsalted butter, melted

1 egg, lightly beaten

In a mixing bowl, stir together the dry ingredients. Make a well in the center and add the remaining ingredients. Stir, starting at the center and gradually mixing in the dry ingredients to make a smooth batter. Cover the bowl and leave it at room temperature for 1 hour, or refrigerate it overnight.

Heat a heavy skillet or griddle and grease it lightly. With a ladle, pour out the batter to make pancakes about 3 inches across, cooking as many at one time as will fit comfortably in the skillet.

Cook the blini until their surfaces are covered with bubbles, about 1 minute. Then flip them with a spatula and cook for 1 minute more.

Serve hot. Guests may drizzle them with a little butter, if they like, then top them with 1 teaspoon or so of caviar and any other garnishes of their choice. Each blini may be folded over by hand to be popped into the mouth.

Makes about 48 blini

Toast Points and Black Bread

Though blini are the ultimate accompaniment to caviar, add to the variety of the table with 2 dozen or so each of toast points and black bread or pumpernickel triangles.

For toast points, cut at least 6 thin slices (about 1/4 inch) from a good quality white loaf. Toast them golden, then trim the crusts off and cut each slice across both diagonals to make 4 small triangles. Present them in a napkin-lined basket. Keep fresh toast points coming in small batches throughout the party.

Similarly, cut thin slices of a good, dense black bread or pumpernickel into 4 small triangles per slice. Leave the bread untoasted and set it out, slices overlapping, on a narrow tray.

Butter

A little melted butter—from 1/2 teaspoon to a teaspoon at most—may be poured over individual blini before they are topped with caviar.

Use sweet butter only; salted butter will conflict with the salty edge of the caviar. Melt 1 cup of butter in a small saucepan over low heat; pour it into a small pitcher or creamer, and keep it warm on a hot plate, ready for guests to dress their individual portions.

Softened butter should also be on hand

to spread on toast or brown bread. Be sure to remove another 2 sticks of butter from the refrigerator at least 30 minutes before guests arrive.

Sour Cream

If your guests wish to, they can top each portion of caviar with a small dollop of sour cream. Set out at least 1 cup of sour cream in an attractive serving dish, with a small spoon to serve up just the right amount.

Crème fraîche—the ever-more-popular French-style lightly soured thick cream—may be substituted for sour cream, or offered alongside it.

For an elegant garnish, lightly grate some fresh lemon zest over the bowls of sour cream or crème fraîche.

Chopped Egg

A light scattering of chopped egg makes a lovely garnish for caviar hors d'oeuvres.

Prepare the garnish a couple of hours before the party. Hard-boil 8 eggs and let them cool. Then peel them, cut them in half and separate the yolks from the whites. With a sharp knife, finely chop the whites and place them in a serving bowl. With a wooden spoon or a pestle, press the yolks through a fine sieve and put them in a separate bowl. Cover both bowls and refrigerate them until serving time.

Snipped Chives

Set out 1 cup or so of snipped fresh chives as another caviar garnish. For the best texture and flavor, they should be cut crosswise into pieces no more than 1/8 inch wide. An easy way to do the job is with kitchen scissors, snipping through as many chives as you can comfortably cut at one time. Or steady a bundle of chives on a cutting board and carefully cut them crosswise with a sharp knife.

Prepare the chives 2 or 3 hours in advance and keep them in a covered bowl in the refrigerator until serving.

Chopped Sweet Onion

As an alternative to chives, offer a bowl of finely chopped onion—about 1 cup in all. Prepare the onion 2 to 3 hours in advance.

To avoid overpowering the caviar, though, use the sweetest onions you can find. Vidalia, Walla Walla and Maui onions are renowned for their sweetness, and you can count on most good supermarkets or produce shops to stock at least one of these varieties. If you can't find one, though, substitute a sweet red onion or the sweetest, mildest brown-skinned onion you can buy.

Lemon Wedges

A squeeze of fresh lemon enhances the briny flavor of caviar.

There are a couple of options for serving the lemon. If you like, an hour or two in advance, cut 6 to 8 medium-size lemons into eighths, using the tip of the knife or a small fork to remove any seeds from the wedges. Arrange the wedges on a serving plate or tray.

Or, you can cut the lemons in half and wrap each half in a piece of cheesecloth, tying the cloth with kitchen string. Each guest can then keep a lemon half at hand on his or her plate, ready to squeeze—seed free—over several portions of caviar.

Don't cut the lemons into the dainty little slices you sometimes see in restaurants. They're awkward and messy, and don't really give satisfactory control over how much lemon actually goes on the food.

Vodka and Champagne

Iced vodka, sipped neat from shot glasses, is the traditional companion to caviar. Buy a good-quality Russian or Scandinavian vodka and, at the very least, put the bottle or bottles in the freezer the night before the party. (Don't worry; the liquor won't expand and crack the bottle.)

The iced vodka will take on a luxuriously syrupy consistency, and will glide down the throat refreshingly. (It's a good idea to keep an eye on your guests, and even to deliver a gentle warning; the ease of sipping iced vodka might otherwise lead them to drink more than they're used to.)

For a stunning presentation, freeze one or more bottles of vodka in blocks of ice—that is, *if* your freezer is tall enough to comfortably hold the bottles upright. You'll need large cans or half-gallon milk cartons about as tall as the vodka bottles. Pour about an inch of water in the bottom of the containers and freeze. Then center one vodka bottle inside each container and fill them with water almost to the top, and freeze solid. Just as the party begins, dip the containers in hot water to loosen them; slip them off and wrap each block of ice surrounding the bottles with a large linen napkin to catch drips and offer a steady grip for pouring. Place the bottles on a rimmed tray to catch water, and be prepared to change the napkins several times during the party as the ice melts.

Have champagne on hand as well. If you like, and the occasion warrants it, go for a good vintage French champagne or California sparkling wine. Whatever you pour, be sure it's an extra-dry or brut wine, with a crisp, dry edge and fine bubbles that cleanse and refresh the palate for that next bite of caviar.

Sources

© Carol Simowitz

Lamb's Farm
P.O. Box 520
Libertyville, IL 60048
(708) 362-4636
*cheeses, breads, and other
gourmet items*

Maison E. H. Glass, Inc.
111 East 58th St.
New York, NY 10022
(212) 755-3316
caviar and specialty foods

Fitz-Henri Fine Foods
2901 Bayview Ave.
Willowdale, ONT M2K 1E6
Canada
(416) 225-4175
gourmet foods

Susan Green's California Cuisine
3501 Taylor Dr.
Ukiah, CA 94582
(800) 753-8558
specialty foods

The Honey Hollow
277A St. Jean Rd.
Pointe Claire, Quebec H4R 3J1
(514) 697-5153
specialty foods

Kendall Cheese Company
P.O. Box 686
Atascadero, CA 93423
(805) 466-7252
fresh goat cheeses

Manganaro Foods
488 Ninth Ave.
New York, NY 10018
(212) 563-7748
Italian specialties

Marcel et Henri
415 Browning Way
South San Francisco, CA 94080
(415) 871-4230
pâtés and sausages

Maytag Dairy Farms
P.O. Box 806
Newton, IA 50208
(800) 247-2458
Maytag blue cheese

Norm Thompson Outfitters, Inc.
P.O. Box 3999
Portland, OR 97208
(800) 547-1160
smoked salmon, cheeses, and other
gourmet items

Nueske Hillcrest Farm Meats
R.R. 2
Witenberg, WI 54499
(800) 382-2266
hams, bacon, and sausages

Oak Grove Smokehouse, Inc.
17618 Old Jefferson Highway
Prairieville, LA 70769
(504) 673-6857
Cajun andouille and tasso

Paprikas Weiss
1572 Second Ave.
New York, NY 10028
(212) 288-6117
Eastern European specialties

The Serving Spoon
382 Bloor St. West
Toronto, ONT M5S 1X2
(416) 967-7666
gourmet foods

Tillamook County Creamery
 Association
P.O. Box 313
Tillamook, OR 97141
(503) 842-4481
Tillamook cheddar cheese

Totem Smokehouse
1906 Pike Place
Seattle, WA 98101
(800) 9 SALMON
smoked salmon

Walla Walla Gardener's Assocation
210 North 11th Ave.
Walla Walla, WA 99362
(509) 525-7070
sweet Walla Walla onions

Williams-Sonoma
P.O. Box 7456
San Francisco, CA 94210-7456
(800) 541-2233
specialty foods and gourmet cookware

Zabar's
2245 Broadway
New York, NY 10024
(212) 787-2000
specialty foods